Women, Beware the Devil

Lulu Raczka

T0041911

methuen | drama

LONDON • NEW YORK • OXFORD • NEW DELHI • SYDNEY

METHUEN DRAMA
Bloomsbury Publishing Plc
50 Bedford Square, London, WC1B 3DP, UK
1385 Broadway, New York, NY 10018, USA
29 Earlsfort Terrace, Dublin 2, Ireland

BLOOMSBURY, METHUEN DRAMA and the Methuen
Drama logo are trademarks of Bloomsbury Publishing Plc

First published in Great Britain 2023

Cover photograph: Alison Oliver, photographed by Felicity McCabe

Cover concept by Émilie Chen

A catalogue record for this book is available from the British Library.

A catalog record for this book is available from the Library of Congress.

ISBN: PB: 978-1-3504-1402-0
ePDF: 978-1-3504-1403-7
eBook: 978-1-3504-1404-4

Series: Modern Plays

Typeset by Mark Heslington Ltd, Scarborough, North Yorkshire

To find out more about our authors and books visit
www.bloomsbury.com and sign up for our newsletters.

Alison Oliver | Agnes

Theatre includes: *Summer and Smoke*, *The Merchant of Venice*, *Blood Wedding* (The Lir).

Television includes: *Best Interests*, *Conversations with Friends*.

Aurora Dawson-Hunte | Joan

Theatre includes: *Dmitry* (The Marylebone Theatre); *The Mirror and the Light* (RSC); *Mrs Klein*, *Three Winters*, *The House of Bernarda Alba*, *Stuff Happens*, *The Country Wife*, *Trojan Women*, *Twelfth Night*, *As You Like It*, *Cat on a Hot Tin Roof*, *The Changeling*, *The Thickness of Skin* (RADA); *The Government Inspector* (Bridewell Theatre/ Edinburgh Fringe); *Cherry Orchard, Chekhov's Baby* (Oxford University Dramatic Society); *The Proposal*, *The Bear* (Yaroslavl'State Demidov); *School Journey to the Centre of the Earth* (National Theatre Connections/The Old Vic).

Film includes: *Morning Song*.

Television includes: *October Faction*, *The Stranger*, *There She Goes*, *Sex Education*, *Ride Out*, *My Insta Scammer Friend*.

Radio includes: *The Panopticon*.

Other work includes: *Persistence Exile*.

Aurora has also worked on various voice over and audio projects with Prime Solutions, Hachette, Penguin Audible, BBC and Big Finish Productions.

Carly-Sophia Davies | Anna

For the Almeida: *Spring Awakening*.

Theatre includes: *Pavilion* (Theatr Clwyd).

Film includes: *Joanna Hoggs' The Eternal Daughter*, *The Sin Eater*, *Arwel's House*, *Manipulations*.

Television includes: *Midsomer Murders*.

Ioanna Kimbook | Katherine

For the Almeida: *"Daddy" A Melodrama*, *The Duchess of Malfi*.

Theatre includes: *Bitter Wheat* (West End); *Much Ado About Nothing* (National Theatre).

Film includes: *Choose or Die*.

Television includes: *Inside No. 9*, *Flatmates*, *Wedding Season*.

Leo Bill | Edward

For the Almeida: *The Duchess of Malfi*, *The Tragedy of King Richard the Second*.

Theatre includes: *Mephisto [A Rhapsody]*, *Dear Elizabeth* (Gate Theatre); *Curtains* (Rose Theatre Kingston); *A Midsummer Night's Dream*, *The Glass Menagerie* (Young Vic); *Hamlet*, *School for Scandal* (Barbican); *Light Shining in Buckinghamshire*, *A Woman Killed with Kindness* (National Theatre); *Secret Theatre* (Lyric Hammersmith); *The Silence of the Sea* (Donmar Warehouse); *Posh* (Royal Court/West End).

Film includes: *Flux Gourmet*, *Cruella*, *Rare Beasts*, *Peterloo*, *In Fabric*, *Alice Through the Looking Glass*, *Mr Turner*, *A Long Way Down*, *The Girl with the Dragon Tattoo*, *Kinky Boots*, *Vera Drake*, *28 Days Later*, *Gosford Park*.

Television includes: *Funny Woman*, *Becoming Elizabeth*, *War of the Worlds*, *The Long Song*, *Strike*, *Taboo*, *The White Queen*, *Pramface*, *The Borgias*, *Words of Captain Scott*, *Doctor Who*, *Home Time*, *Ashes to Ashes*, *Lead Balloon*, *Sense and Sensibility*, *Jekyll*, *Bash*, *A Very Social Secretary*, *Silent Witness*, *Messiah III*, *Beethoven's Eroica*, *The Canterbury Tales*, *Spooks*, *Midsomer Murders*, *Surrealismo*, *Attachments II*, *Crime and Punishment*.

Lola Shalam | Mary

Lola is in her final year at Guildhall School of Music and Drama and *Women, Beware the Devil* is her professional stage debut.

Lydia Leonard | Elizabeth

For the Almeida: *Little Eyolf.*

Theatre includes: *The Meeting* (Chichester Festival Theatre); *Oslo* (National Theatre/West End); *Wolf Hall* (RSC/Broadway, Tony Award nomination for Best Featured Actress in a Play); *Onassis* (West End); *Time and the Conways* (National Theatre); *Let There Be Love* (Tricycle Theatre); *Frost/Nixon* (Donmar Warehouse/West End); *Hecuba* (RSC).

Film includes: *Northern Comfort*, *Last Christmas*, *The Fifth Estate*, *Born of War*, *Legendary*, *Archipelago*, *True True Lie*.

Television includes: *The Crown*, *Ten Percent*, *Gentleman Jack*, *Flesh and Blood*, *Quacks*, *Absentia*, *Apple Tree Yard*, *Life in Squares*, *River*, *Lucan*, *Ambassadors*, *Da Vinci's Demons*, *Whitechapel*, *Law & Order*, *Spooks*, *Casualty 1909*, *The 39 Steps*, *Ashes to Ashes*, *Margaret Thatcher*, *A Line of Beauty*, *Jericho*, *Rome*.

Nathan Armarkwei-Laryea | The Devil

For the Almeida: *Spring Awakening*.

Theatre includes: *Hamlet*, *Faith, Hope and Charity*, *Tartuffe* (National Theatre); *The 306 Dawn* (National Theatre of Scotland); *Her Naked Skin* (Salisbury Playhouse); *Romeo and Juliet* (Exeter Northcott Theatre); *Vernon God Little* (The Space); *Homo Sacer* (The Old Vic 12).

Film includes: *In Darkness*, *Hunting Sublime*, *Oegs*.

Television includes: *The Witcher*, *Doctors*, *Doctor Who*.

As a writer, Nathan is co-writing his first television series, a black comedy, in development at Drama Republic.

Adam Cork | Sound Designer and Composer

Adam is composer and co-lyricist of the documentary musical *London Road* which had an extended run at the National Theatre Cottesloe before transferring to the Olivier auditorium. He received a Tony Award in 2010 for his music and sound score for *Red* (Donmar Warehouse/ Broadway) and an Olivier Award in 2011 for *King Lear* (Donmar Warehouse). Adam received the 2011 Evening Standard Award 'Best Design' for *Anna Christie* and *King Lear* (Donmar Warehouse) and the 2011 Critics' Circle 'Best Musical' for *London Road*. He was also nominated in 2010 for the Tony Award 'Best Score (Music & Lyrics)' for *ENRON* (Broadway/West End).

For the Almeida: *Patriots*, *The Hunt*, *Ink* (also West End/Broadway).

Theatre includes: *The 47th* (The Old Vic); *The Shark is Broken*, *Leopoldstadt*, *Who's Afraid of Virginia Woolf?*, *No Man's Land*, *Photograph 51*, *Don Carlos*, *Suddenly Last Summer* (West End); *Travesties* (Menier Chocolate Factory/West End/Broadway); *Les Blancs*, *Three Days in the Country* (National Theatre); *Frost/Nixon* (Donmar Warehouse/West End/Broadway); *Ivanov* (Donmar Warehouse/West End); *The Chalk Garden*, *Creditors*, *The Wild Duck*, *Caligula* (Donmar Warehouse).

Film includes: *Genius*, *London Road*.

Television includes: *The Hollow Crown*, *Macbeth*, *Frances Tuesday*, *Re-ignited*, *Imprints*.

Alice Townes | Wigs, Hair and Makeup Supervisor

For the Almeida: *The Twilight Zone* (West End).

Theatre includes: As Head of Wigs and Makeup: *Hairspray The Musical* (London Coliseum); *9 to 5: The Musical* (UK tour); *The Color Purple* (Curve Theatre, Leicester); *Don Quixote* (West End); *Little Shop Of Horrors* (Regent's Park Open Air Theatre); *Girl From The North Country* (The Old Vic).

As Deputy Head of Wigs and Makeup: *The Sound of Music* (International tour); *Harry Potter and The Cursed Child* (West End).

As Deputy Head of Wigs: *Hamilton*, *Beautiful – The Carole King Musical* (West End); *Dirty Rotten Scoundrels* (West End/UK tour).

Television includes: As Crowd Hair and Makeup Supervisor: *The Witcher – Blood Origin*.

As Core Crowd Hair and Makeup Artist: *The Witcher*.

As Hair and Makeup Artist: *Sport Relief*, *Siblings*, *Uncle*.

Amy Ball | Casting Director

For the Almeida: *"Daddy" A Melodrama*, *Albion*, *The Hunt*, *Shipwreck*, *Dance Nation*, *Boy*.

Theatre includes: *Uncle Vanya*, *Leopoldstadt*, *The Night of the Iguana*, *Rosmersholm*, *Who's Afraid of Virginia Woolf?* (West End); *The Son* (Kiln Theatre/West End); *Sweat* (Donmar Warehouse/West End); *A Very Very Dark Matter* (Bridge Theatre); *Exit the King*, *Consent* (National Theatre); *On Bear Ridge*, *Glass. Kill. Bluebeard. Imp*, *White Pearl*, *The Cane*, *ear for eye*, *Girls and Boys*, *The Children*, *road*, *Anatomy of a Suicide*, *The Ferryman*, *Cyprus Avenue*, *X*, *Hangmen*, *Escaped Alone*, *Linda*, *Liberian Girl*, *How to Hold Your Breath*, *Constellations*, *Jumpy*, *Posh*, *The River* (Royal Court); *Jerusalem* (Royal Court/West End); *Measure for Measure* (Young Vic); *The Moderate Soprano* (Hampstead Theatre).

Dubheasa Lanipekun | Assistant Director

Dubheasa Lanipekun (she/her) is a multidisciplinary theatremaker, filmmaker and photographer. In her lens-based practice she was most recently a Sundance Institute Fellow on the Ignite Programme with Adobe, winning a place with her debut short film *Blue Corridor 15* (Dazed/ICA/BBC). Her work is motivated by finding the social truth within drama. She is interested in work which revolves around and interrogates the theme of liberation. Her practice is grounded in a deep interest in the politicised lives of people.

Theatre includes: As Director: *Bone* (Omnibus Theatre); *Deb & Joan* (Canal Café Theatre); *Blind Date* (Katzpace); *A.I. in Wonderland* (University of Warwick).

As Assistant Director: *Paradise Now!* (Bush Theatre); *Handbagged* (Kiln Theatre); *WE NEED TO TALK ABOUT GRIEF* (Donmar Warehouse).

As Assistant Dramaturg: *Clean Break Pathways Programme* (Royal Court).

Evie Gurney | Costume Designer

For the Almeida: *The Hunt.*

Theatre includes: *Antony and Cleopatra, Much Ado About Nothing* (National Theatre); *The 47th* (The Old Vic); *The Seagull* (Dramaten, Stockholm); *Much Ado About Nothing* (Shakespeare Theatre Company, Washington DC).

Imogen Knight | Movement Director and Intimacy Co-ordinator

For the Almeida: *The Tragedy of King Richard the Second, Against, Carmen Disruption, Little Revolution, The Turn of the Screw, King Lear, Filumena, Measure for Measure, When the Rain Stops Falling.*

Theatre includes: *Good, Walden, Uncle Vanya, Rosmersholm, The Birthday Party, Who's Afraid of Virginia Woolf?* (West End); *Future Frequencies* (Esch 2022); *The Wife of Willesden* (Kiln Theatre); *Is God Is, The Song Project, Bodies, Fake News, Linda, God Bless The Child, The Low Road* (Royal Court); *Under Milk Wood* (National Theatre); *The Son* (Kiln Theatre/West End); *The Half God of Rainfall* (Fuel Theatre/ Kiln Theatre/Birmingham Rep); *Blood Wedding, Jesus Hopped the 'A' Train, The Emperor* (Young Vic).

As Movement Director and Intimacy Co-ordinator: *The Welkin* (National Theatre).

As Movement Consultant: *The Christians* (LAMDA).

As Intimacy Co-ordinator: *Romeo and Julie, Jekyll & Hyde* (National Theatre).

As Director: *Nuclear War* (Royal Court).

Opera includes: *The Handmaid's Tale, The Winter's Tale, Powder Her Face* (ENO); *The Knife of Dawn* (Royal Opera House); *Flux, Rush Hour 10: Motion* (Southbank Sinfonia); *Gazelle Twin & NYX* (Ovalhouse/Southbank Centre).

Film includes: *Embers, The Bubble.*

Television includes: *The Power.*

Jonathan Holby | Fight Director

For the Almeida: *A Streetcar Named Desire, The Duchess of Malfi, Summer and Smoke* (also West End); *Machinal.*

Theatre includes: *The Lion, the Witch and the Wardrobe, Cabaret, Ghost Stories, Waitress, The King and I, Killer Joe, The Spoils, Strictly Ballroom* (West End); *Orfeus: A House Music Opera* (Young Vic); *The Way of the World* (Donmar Warehouse); *Oslo* (National Theatre/West End); *Oliver Twist* (Regent's Park Open Air Theatre); *The Wild Party* (The Other Palace); *The Trial of Jane Fonda* (Park Theatre); *Romeo and Juliet, Hamlet, Twelfth Night, The Tempest, Macbeth, A Midsummer Night's Dream* (Shakespeare's Rose Theatre); *Private Peaceful, Holes, Lit, Coram Boy, The Madness of George III, The Memory of Water* (Nottingham Playhouse); *Richard II* (The Vaults); *The Be All and End All, Robin Hood* (York Theatre Royal).

Film includes: *Black Dog, Tuesday, Tiny Dancer, Swing for the Fences, Amaranthine, The Mother, the Son, the Rat and the Gun, Damned, Protectors of the Dawn, My Mother, Work.*

Lulu Raczka | Writer

Theatre includes: *Gulliver's Travels* (Unicorn Theatre); *Antigone* (New Diorama Theatre); *A Girl in School Uniform (Walks into a Bar)* (West Yorkshire Playhouse/New Diorama Theatre); *Grey Man* (Shoreditch Festival/Theatre503); *Clytemnestra* (Gate Theatre); *Some People Talk About Violence* (Edinburgh Fringe/New Diorama Theatre/Camden People's Theatre); *Nothing* (Summerhall/Lyric Hammersmith/Warwick Arts Centre/Camden People's Theatre, The Sunday Times Playwriting Award, the National Student Drama Festival Award for Creative Risk).

Television includes: *Riviera, Medici: Masters of Florence.*

Radio includes: *Of a Lifetime* (2019 Imison Award).

Miriam Buether | Set Designer

For the Almeida as Designer: *Patriots, Spring Awakening, Hymn, Albion, Shipwreck, Machinal, Boy, Game, When the Rain Stops Falling, Judgement Day.*

Theatre and Dance as Designer includes: *The 47th* (The Old Vic); *King Lear, To Kill a Mockingbird, Three Tall Women, A Doll's House 2, The Children* (Broadway); *The Jungle* (Young Vic/West End/St Ann's Warehouse); *The Trial, Public Enemy, Wild Swans, The Government Inspector, The Good Soul of Szechuan, Generations, Measure for Measure* (Young Vic); *Glass. Kill. Blubeard. Imp., Sucker Punch, Cock, In the Republic of Happiness, Get Santa!* (Royal Court); *The Children,*

Escaped Alone, *Love and Information* (Royal Court/Minetta Lane Theatre); *Sunny Afternoon*, *Bend it Like Beckham* (West End); *Chariots of Fire* (Hampstead Theatre/West End); *The Father* (Theatre Royal Bath); *The Effect*, *Earthquakes in London* (National Theatre).

Opera as Designer includes: *La Fanciulla Del West* (ENO/Santa Fe Opera); *Turandot*, *Wozzeck* (ENO); *Aida, Suor Angelica* (Royal Opera House, as Set Designer); *Anna Nicole* (Royal Opera House/BAM, New York); Boris Godunov (Berlin Opera).

Miriam received the Evening Standard Best Design Award in 2010 for *Earthquakes in London* and *Sucker Punch*, and in 2018 for *The Jungle*.

Peter Todd | Costume Supervisor

For the Almeida: *"Daddy" A Melodrama*, *The Hunt*.

Theatre and Dance includes: As Costume Designer: *Double Murder* (Hofesh Shechter Company); *Voices and Light Footsteps*, *Chacony* (Richard Alston Dance Company); *The Waiting Game* (Ballet Black); *The Snow Queen*, *Hansel and Gretel*, *Alice in Winterland* (Rose Theatre Kingston); *Frankenstein* (Aquilla Theatre).

As Costume Supervisor: *The Rape of Lucretia*, *La Traviata*, *Salome* (Royal Opera House); *The Lost Thing* (Candoco/Royal Opera House); *Flight Pattern*, *Unearthed*, *Don Quixote* (The Royal Ballet); *Lest We Forget*, *Le Corsaire* (English National Ballet); *Stories*, *As You Like It* (National Theatre); *Julius Caesar* (Bridge Theatre); *Prisoner of the State*, *Dead Man Walking* (Barbican); *People, Places and Things* (Headlong); *A Pacifist's Guide to the War on Cancer* (Complicité).

Rupert Goold | Director

Artistic Director of the Almeida Theatre, founding Artistic Director of Headlong (2005 to 2013); Associate Director at the RSC and Artistic Director of Northampton Theatres (2002 to 2005).

For the Almeida: *Tammy Faye*, *Patriots*, *Spring Awakening*, *Albion*, *The Hunt*, *Shipwreck*, *Richard III*, *Medea*, *The Merchant of Venice*, *The Last Days of Judas Iscariot*, *American Psycho* (also Broadway); *Ink*, *King Charles III* (also West End/Broadway).

Theatre includes: *The 47th* (The Old Vic); *The Effect*, *Earthquakes in London* (Headlong/National Theatre); *Time and the Conways* (National Theatre); *The Lion, the Witch and the Wardrobe* (Kensington

Gardens); *The Merchant of Venice*, *Romeo and Juliet*, *Speaking Like Magpies* (RSC); *ENRON* (Headlong/West End/Broadway); *Made in Dagenham*, *Oliver!*, *The Glass Menagerie*, *No Man's Land* (West End); *King Lear* (Headlong/Liverpool Everyman/Young Vic); *Six Characters in Search of an Author* (Headlong/West End); *Macbeth* (Chichester Festival Theatre/West End/Broadway).

Film includes: *Judy*, *True Story*.

Television includes: *Macbeth*, *King Charles III*, *Richard II*.

Opera includes: *Turandot* (ENO); *Le Comte Ory* (Garsington Opera).

Rupert has received Olivier, Critics' Circle and Evening Standard awards for Best Director twice and won a Peabody Award in 2011 for *Macbeth*. Rupert received a CBE in 2017 New Year's Honours for services to drama.

Tim Lutkin | Lighting Designer

For the Almeida: *The Tragedy of Macbeth*, *Chimerica* (also West End, Olivier Award for Best Lighting Design).

Theatre includes: *Back To The Future: The Musical*, *Fiddler on the Roof*, *Life of Pi* (UK Theatre Award for Best Design and Olivier Award for Best Lighting Design); *Four Quartets*, *Big*, *Noises Off*, *Elf*, *Quiz*, *The Girls*, *The Go Between*, *Close To You*, *Impossible*, *Strangers on a Train*, *The Full Monty* (West End); *The Crucible*, *Under Milk Wood*, *Anthony and Cleopatra*, *Salomé*, *Les Blancs* (National Theatre); *Timon of Athens*, *The Rover*, *Candide*, *All's Well That Ends Well* (RSC); *Lungs*, *Present Laughter*, *The Crucible* (The Old Vic).

Other work includes: *The Lion King*, *Mickey and the Magician*, *Marvel Superheroes*, *Frozen Celebration*, *Disney Junior Dream Factory* (Walt Disney Imagineering).

Supported by the *Women, Beware the Devil* Production Syndicate and the Genesis Founation's Genesis Kickstart Fund.

Almeida Theatre

The Almeida Theatre makes brave new work that asks big questions: of plays, of theatre and of the world around us. Whether new work or reinvigorated classics, the Almeida brings together the most exciting artists to take risks; to provoke, inspire and surprise our audiences.

Since 2013, the Almeida has been led by Artistic Director Rupert Goold and Executive Director Denise Wood.

Recent highlights include Associate Director Rebecca Frecknall's production of *A Streetcar Named Desire*, featuring Patsy Ferran, Paul Mescal and Anjana Vasan; Rupert Goold's productions of *Tammy Faye*, a new musical from Elton John, Jake Shears and James Graham; Peter Morgan's *Patriots* and Steven Sater and Duncan Sheik's musical *Spring Awakening*; Danya Taymor's production of Jeremy O. Harris' *"Daddy"* and Yaël Farber's production of *The Tragedy of Macbeth*.

Previous productions include Rupert Goold's Olivier Award-winning productions of James Graham's *Ink* (transferred to the West End and Broadway) and Mike Bartlett's *King Charles III* (transferred to West End and Broadway and adapted for BBC television); Rebecca Frecknall's Olivier Award-winning production of Tennessee Williams' *Summer and Smoke* (transferred to West End); Robert Icke's productions of *Hamlet* and *Oresteia* (both of which ran earlier this year at Park Avenue Armory in New York) and *Mary Stuart* (West End and UK tour); and Lyndsey Turner's Olivier Award-winning production of Lucy Kirkwood's *Chimerica*.

Women, Beware the Devil

Notes on the Text

Design and Setting

This is set in the early/middle of the seventeenth century. The period can be taken as seriously as you want for design.

Historical Accuracy

The family presented in the play are completely invented. In the backdrop of the play the events leading up to the Civil War are playing out. These events are all described truthfully, well, truthfully from the biased perspective of our characters, who are mostly firm Royalists. However, sometimes the space in which these events occurred has been blurred to serve the drama.

Performance

The dialogue is often broken down over many lines of text. This is not to show hesitation, but the natural flow of speaking, the lines ending as the thought changes. Do not think you have to pause at the end of every line, it should flow.

Formatting

Due to the nature of the house – of their being servants, and their superiors, and due to larger scenes, of multiple situations at once, sometimes there are two conversations happening at once. This will be demonstrated as follows –

> *The conversation that is happening out of the hearing of the other conversation will happen indented like this.*

Characters

Main

Elizabeth, *lady of the house, sister of Edward.*
Agnes, *servant.*
Katherine, *lady of the house, wife of Edward. For casting, she should be around the same age as* **Agnes**.
Edward, *the Earl. For casting, I would suggest around the same age as* **Elizabeth**, *maybe a little younger.*
Joan, *servant. Older than* **Agnes**.
Anna, *servant. Younger/same age as* **Agnes**.
Mary, *servant.*
The Devil, *whatever you want.*

Other

The **Devil** *should multi-role as all other male characters, so the* **Physician**, *the* **Witchfinder**, *the* **Artist**, **Francis**

Induction

The Devil   Gosh, these days.

These days!

Tough – aren't they?

You feel it – don't you?

Everything feels like it's –

I don't know . . .

Crumbling, somehow.

Strikes, governmental implosions –

It's the seventies all over again –

Except this time everyone is staring at their
phones –

Almost every newspaper delivering front page
tirades –

About letting people drown in the sea –

While every billion-dollar company is covered
in rainbows –

What's real?

Is everything getting better?

Or much, much worse?

Almost makes you want to dial up your
doctor –

And get yourself sectioned –

But good luck getting an appointment.

And yet you never thank *me* for any of it!

'Cause in the old days –

People would look around at all this –

And they'd say –

This is the work of the devil!

But now no –

No, no, no –

Now –

It's systemic –

Structural –

Patriarchal –

But no –

Never evil!

So I suppose my work here is done.

Evil has adapted.

You don't need me anymore.

But I do miss the old days

When I really did strike terror –

Into the heart of any decent Englishman –

So I'm taking you there with me –

Back to the seventeenth century –

Up north, a war is happening in Scotland over a prayer book –

And in London –

Very noble men are challenging the King –

Peccant Hall now comes into view behind him. January 1640. A woman stands there – the **Lady Elizabeth de Clare**.

The Devil   But here, in Peccant Hall –

The Lady Elizabeth de Clare has her own problems.

The **Devil** *hands* **Elizabeth** *a pamphlet.*

The Devil   So I'll leave you here –

Enjoy the play –

It's pretty long –

But don't worry –

There's a lot to enjoy –

Seductions and betrayals –

Temptations and terror –

And for all you perverts –

There'll be sex and violence –

And I know you guys don't like spoilers –

But by the end of the play a witch will be hanged –

And the whole family will be murdered!

So it's worth sticking around for

Enjoy!

Act I

Scene One

Elizabeth *stands across from a young woman,* **Agnes**, *who is dressed in the lowest clothes, covered in mud.*

Elizabeth	It's Agnes, isn't it?
	Agnes Albyn?
Agnes	Is this about Bessie?
Elizabeth	Who?
Agnes	The cow.
	They say I killed her.
Elizabeth	And did you?
Agnes	If I wanted to kill Bessie I'd take a knife to her throat –
	I wouldn't use spells and potions.
Elizabeth	But my staff tell me you like spells and potions.
	That you like the Devil even.
	And keep them up at night calling out to him.
Agnes	And what do they know about it?
Elizabeth	Sadly we all know a lot about the Devil these days –
	Don't we?
	Anyone can read about it in this nasty pamphlet.
	Because it's not just Bessie, is it?
	It's all the cows, the sheep –
	Deer –

The crops –

And when there were cows –

Where there should have been milk –

There was blood.

Agnes   You think I did all that?

Elizabeth *Everyone* thinks you did all that.

Agnes   And can *everyone* explain –

Why some stable girl –

Would start killing herself out of a job?

Elizabeth They say you're jealous or you're angry –

Or just that you're mad.

Any one of those will do for an arrest –

But I would prefer a confession.

So.

Which is it?

Agnes   What's that?

On the wall.

Elizabeth Agnes –

This won't work.

Agnes   Please.

It looks like.

It looks like heaven.

Well.

What I think heaven would be like.

Elizabeth And what's that?

Agnes   You'd think that when God was making his house

He'd think over every little detail –

You see that in nature –

But I've never seen it in anything made by man before

Where everything

Every tiny thing

Is beautiful

Elizabeth   You understand then –

Why I have to do everything I can –

Everything possible –

To protect this house –

And you understand –

Don't you –

What that means for you?

Agnes   I should have known

They'd show you heaven –

Before you go to hell –

Elizabeth   Answer me, Agnes.

You understand?

Agnes   I understand.

But I promise –

Those liars out there know nothing –

I am *good*.

I say my prayers every night –

	Go to church every week –
	And I would never hurt this house –
	You've given me work when I needed it –
	And I'm very grateful.
Elizabeth	You don't show it.
Agnes	I show it every day when I work very hard –
	Without ever complaining.
Elizabeth	Then those liars, as you call them –
	Why are they so certain?
Agnes	My mother.
	She did those things.
Elizabeth	Albyn . . .
	I remember now.
	Oh yes, the staff loved a good story about your mother.
	She taught you her ways, I suppose?
Agnes	I would never.
Elizabeth	But you did learn?

Agnes *nods.*

Elizabeth	They're not very nice about you –
	The staff –
	I suppose considering that –
	I understand why you'd do all this –
Agnes	I didn't.
Elizabeth	Shall I tell the Magistrate that?
	You were bullied?
	Cruelty pushed you to it –

Agnes   I didn't do anything.

Nothing!

They are lying!

Elizabeth   Let's imagine I'm your friend –

Your only one, clearly –

I am going to tell you the truth.

We will get a confession from you –

And you will hang –

But what is currently still up to you –

Is whether you give one here –

In this nice, warm room –

With me –

Holding your hand if you wish –

Or –

You give one at the gaol –

And –

As you seem like a girl who has seen her fair
share of the world –

I'm sure you can imagine in what state you'll
give it there.

Agnes   Everyday on this earth I have fought to be
good –

To be as different from my mother as possible –

And if I were to give up on a lifetime's effort –

It wouldn't be to kill some sheep and cows it
would be to –

To –

To –

Elizabeth   To what?

Agnes   I don't know –

But it would be to do something.

Something.

Important.

Elizabeth *thinks*.

Elizabeth   My brother is to be married.

A girl called Katherine Brooker.

She's a sweet girl and I'm sure she'll make a nice mistress.

Agnes   To who?

Elizabeth   You, of course.

Would you like that?

Agnes   What about the gaol?

Elizabeth   Just answer me.

You'd like that?

Agnes   Yes.

Elizabeth   I thought so.

But you see there's a problem.

My brother refuses.

Katherine has no title and he thinks her common.

But he doesn't see –

That Katherine can give us things we need more than titles.

Money.

	And of course –
	An heir.
	So –
	If you want the job –
	You'll help me convince him.
Agnes	And how will I do that?
Elizabeth	Your skills, of course.
	You said it yourself –
	You've always wanted to use them for something important.
	This is your chance.
	So?

A pause while **Agnes** *thinks.*

Agnes	No.
Elizabeth	No?
Agnes	I am good.
Elizabeth	You understand you'll hang?
Agnes	I have to die someday –
	Better to do so knowing I'm not going to hell.
Elizabeth	I thought you wanted to be lady's maid?
Agnes	Very much.
	But not that much.
Elizabeth	This house –
	It's my –
	How did you put it?
	My something important.

But for how much longer?

Because all the money is gone.

And each year –

The repairs mount up –

And the debts with them –

And if this continues –

I'll have to turn to my cousin Henry –

Or other distant family –

For help.

And they'll have conditions –

And I could soon be sat here in this room –

Feigning gratitude –

As I watch these people –

Destroy the place I'd given up everything for.

Agnes   Who would destroy this house?

Elizabeth   They wouldn't do it with purpose –

But with a lack of true belief in all it could be.

But if my brother marries –

And has a son.

They'll never get near it.

Agnes   You'd need to give something in return.

Elizabeth   Like what?

Agnes   Blood.

And there's no telling if it'll take more after.

Outside, the servants clean. **Joan,** *clearly the leader, and* **Anna**
and **Mary**.

Mary	A hanging?!
	No.
	No way.
Joan	Mary.
	I'm telling you.
	The mistress comes over all huffed –
	Calling out Joan! Joan!
	Bring me that girl who you all call a witch –
Mary	That doesn't mean anything.
Joan	Oh yes it does.
	She'd just been sent a pamphlet.
	From London.
Mary	What did it say?
Anna	Ohhhh please.
	Don't.
Mary	Scared the witch'll put spiders in your bed?
Anna	Do they do that?
Mary	Yes –
	But magic spiders –
Anna	No . . .
Mary	That climb into the whites of your eyes to make their webs –
Anna	Noooooo.
Joan	Mary.
	Who was it that woke me up in the middle of the night –

Wailing –

Over a witch getting into your dreams?

Anna   Can they do that?

Joan   Anna.

The mistress is in there right now –

Getting our witch all ready for her hanging –

You don't have to be scared anymore.

Anna   I don't want to see it.

Joan   I do.

Mary   You shouldn't watch when they fall –

My mum says if you see a witch die –

She'll haunt you from hell.

Anna *puts her hands over her ears.* **Elizabeth** *leads* **Agnes** *out into the hall where the women are speaking.*

Elizabeth   Joan.

Find space for Agnes.

She'll be living in the house from now on.

And train her.

She'll be a lady's maid.

Joan, **Mary** *and* **Anna** *stare at them, shocked . . .*

Joan   Lady's maid to who, My Lady?

Elizabeth   You'll find out soon enough.

Elizabeth *leads* **Agnes** *away.*

Mary   I told you.

Anna   But maybe it's just because she's not the witch –

If anyone would know –

Joan   Agnes?

A lady's maid?

Mary   If you gave that girl face powder –

She'd eat it with a comb.

Joan   This is witchcraft plain as day . . .

Elizabeth *turns to the audience and addresses them directly.*

Elizabeth   I wish you didn't have to see the house like
this.

It really is the best house in the country.

Imagine.

The Great Hall –

About two –

No. Let's say four times the size of theatre
you're in –

Portraits lining the walls of my father and
grandfathers –

Going all the way back to the boats from
Normandy –

And from the outside –

It's a fortress –

Sieges on this house have lasted years.

I could give you the history lessons –

I've heard them my whole life.

They were more for my brother than me –

I was supposed to marry and leave –

But by accident or not –

I fell in love with it all.

And stayed.

And why shouldn't I?

I understand it!

And these days –

It doesn't feel like many do.

I wonder –

Do you?

Are you looking back in horror –

At what you believe you've outgrown?

Or with tears –

At everything you let slip away?

Or maybe you're looking back with gratitude –

Screaming through the veil –

Thank you!

You did it!

You kept it all alive!

That's what I have to hope for –

Because it's a lot –

Isn't it?

My soul –

For the house?

An eternity in hell –

Just so these bricks might stay together half as long.

Please.

Let it be worth it.

Elizabeth *cuts her wrist . . .*

Scene Two

Edward *has married* **Katherine**, *and the family sit down to dinner on their wedding night, while* **Agnes**, **Joan**, **Anna** *and* **Mary** *serve them.*

Katherine *is young and pretty. She and* **Edward** *wear formal clothes. She wears clothes more 'in fashion' than* **Elizabeth**, *but she is not comfortable in them. She does not have the ease, the entitlement.*

They eat their first course.

Edward	I just don't know when it happened –
	But everyone decided that everything that was –
	Isn't anymore –
	One day –
	The King is the King –
Elizabeth	As he is.
Edward	And the sky is blue –
	The grass is green –
	And the dew settles in the morning –
	But now people ask –
	Do we really think the sky should be blue?
	And are we sure it really is blue in the first place?
	How could we ever know if it was anyway?
	And when I say –
	Stick your head out of the window –
	And look up –
	It makes me an idiot!
	I thought we were having beef this evening.

Joan *speaks to* **Agnes**.

Joan	Yes Agnes,
	Where is all the beef?
Agnes	Stop it.
Edward	And I said it.
	I stood up and said –
	The King is the King –
	Because he is!
	The King is the King is the King is the King –
	Is the King!
	And I swear it –
	He looked at me –
Elizabeth	I am sure he did, brother.
Edward	I was looking the other way –
	But I saw him –
	In the corner of my eye –
	Smiling.
	Is there no way they could get some beef now?
	I'll wait.

Edward *notices* **Katherine**. *He jumps, scared, as if he has never seen her before. A long pause . . . He leans into* **Elizabeth**.

Edward	Who is that?
Elizabeth	Brother. Is this a joke?

But he is serious. **Elizabeth** *stares at* **Agnes**, *worried*.

Elizabeth	That's your wife.
	Katherine.
	Remember?

Edward   My . . .

Elizabeth   You really don't remember?

Elizabeth *grabs* **Agnes**, *and whispers.*

>   **Elizabeth**   What's wrong with him?

Agnes *shakes her head, not knowing.* **Edward** *looks around at all the women in the room, who all look at him as if he is crazy. He laughs, falsely.*

Edward   Of course I remember!

He turns to **Katherine**.

>   So *my love.*
>
>   Tell me –
>
>   Do you like beef?

Elizabeth   *Edward.*

Edward   No, no sister –
>
>   I really think we deserve it –
>
>   Tonight.
>
>   Being our wedding night.
>
>   Don't you agree –

Edward *stumbles, trying to remember her name.*

Elizabeth   *Katherine.*

Edward   Katherine –
>
>   You'd like beef on your wedding –
>
>   Wouldn't you?

Katherine *is about to speak. Second course is served.*

Edward   Fish.
>
>   Fish?

Joan	Yes, sir.
Elizabeth	You know, brother –
	You should ask Katherine about her father –
	He hates those men in Parliament as much as you do –
Edward	Fish are silver.
	They swim in the sea.
	I wanted beef.
	Beef comes from cows.
	They walk on land.
	Usually a mix of black and white.
Joan	I know, Sir –
Edward	Well if you know what a cow is –
	Why is one not lying dead in front of me?
Elizabeth	Brother –
Joan	Yes, Agnes, why?

Agnes *elbows* **Joan** *in the stomach.* **Joan** *drops a plate.*

Edward *turns to her.*

Edward	What is wrong *now?*
Agnes	Nothing, Sir.
	An accident.
Joan	No accident, Sir.
	The witch got me.
	Didn't she?
Anna	*Don't.*
Mary	She did! I saw it.

Anna   *Mary.*

Elizabeth   Joan.

Katherine   There's a witch . . .?

Joan   Yes, My Lady –

                  That's why there's no beef –

Elizabeth   *Joan.*

Joan *steps back in line.*

Edward   A witch?

Elizabeth   Don't tempt them.

Edward   I want to hear it, sister.

Elizabeth *looks at* **Agnes** *worried – are they caught?*

Joan   They say there's a witch, Sir.

                  She came for the crops.

                  Then the cows and the deer.

                  And now she's coming for us –

                  Isn't she, Agnes?

Edward   Who's been telling you all this?

Elizabeth   It's lies, brother.

                  You can't listen to them.

Edward   *They say* there's a witch.

                  That's what you said –

                  They say.

                  Who says?

Joan   Here. In town.

                  Everyone.

	People's crops are dying –
	And they want to know why!
Mary	They're scared is all, Sir.
	We're all scared.
	Aren't we?
Anna	Yeah. We are, Sir.
Joan	We need a Witchfinder, Sir –
	We need someone to come here and catch her –
	Whoever she is!
Edward	Enough!
	Enough.

Edward *pauses, thinking.* **Elizabeth** *looks at* **Agnes**, *worried.*

Edward	This is them.
	It's those men in London.
	They've seen me –
	Proud supporter of our King –
	And so they say this!
	Think how happy they'd be if we sent for a Witchfinder?
	Some Puritan freak sniffing through our linens –
	And declaring us of the Devil!
	Enough of this –
	All of it!
	Enough.

Edward *storms out.*

Scene Three

In **Katherine***'s room,* **Agnes** *brushes* **Katherine***'s hair.*

Katherine	I've heard that you're new?
	That makes me happy.
	Everything here is so old –
	And so clever –
	Isn't my husband clever?
Agnes	Yes, Mistress, very.
Katherine	I couldn't understand a word he was saying.
	It was just so, very clever.
	But I'm glad that you're new.
	That means we can be friends, yes?
Agnes	*Friends?*
Katherine	Yes –
	Friends!
	Unless you don't want to be my friend?
Agnes	No –
	My Lady –
	Of course.
Katherine	So as a friend.
	You must tell me what happens now?
Agnes	Now?
Katherine	Between man and wife.
Agnes	I'm not married, Mistress.
Katherine	But my sister says servant girls have all the best advice.

Agnes	Aren't your sisters married?
	What did they tell you?
Katherine	Beatrice said to close my eyes –
	Count to ten backwards in my head
	And that –
	Whatever I do –
	I must not weep.
	Margaret says that I'll enjoy it –
	But I must not let on that I enjoy it –
	Or I lose all the bargaining power –
	Whatever that means.
Agnes	I don't think your sisters are very helpful.
Katherine	No.
	Come on –
	You must know something –
	As a friend?
Agnes	I do know one thing.
	What a man has between his legs?
	I suppose you've seen what a dog has?
Katherine	Dogs!
	I think we're far from those creatures.
Agnes	In many ways yes –
	In this way I think no –
Katherine	I see.
Agnes	Are you scared?

Katherine   Yes.

But I think it's right to be scared –

Because right now I'm a girl.

But tomorrow I wake up a woman.

A knock at the door.

I'm glad I met you this evening, Agnes,

When I'm a girl –

Because tomorrow we'll already be old friends!

Agnes *leaves.* **Edward** *enters. He pours himself a drink.*

Edward   Would you like one?

Katherine *shakes her head.*

Edward   Vocally, please.

Katherine   No, thank you.

Edward.

Edward   Good.

He sits beside her.

Now that we are –

By all outward evidence –

Husband and wife –

He puts a hand on her leg.

You know what would naturally follow?

She shakes her head. He downs his drink.

Again –

Words, dear.

Katherine   I do not know exactly.

Edward   You don't?

Katherine   But it is not nervousness or fear –

I just.

Haven't been taught.

But I am –

Excited.

To discover.

Edward   As you should be.

Katherine   Are you?

Edward   Am I what?

Katherine   Excited.

Edward   Usually, yes.

I am a man, after all.

Katherine   But not now?

Edward   Let's see, shall we.

He kisses her. She is hesitant, but starts to enjoy herself. He stops.

No. Not now.

He stands up, and starts to leave.

Katherine   I'm sorry.

Edward   What for?

Katherine   Did I do something wrong?

Edward   Not at all.

You've acted your part in this strange day
adequately –

As well as any young girl could hope to –

But it is all a little . . .

Isn't it?

Scene Four

Joan *bangs on* **Katherine**'s *door,* **Mary** *and* **Anna** *stand behind her.*

Joan	My Lady –
	Are you awake?
Anna	Wasn't she beautiful?
	Katherine?
Mary	She was *alright.*
Joan	She's not proper though, is she?
	Not like the Lady Elizabeth –
Anna	She's a lot nicer.
Joan	Her dad is in trade. Like mine.
Mary	Her dad builds ships for the King.
	Your dad sells fish every other Sunday.

Anna *laughs.* **Agnes** *approaches, and* **Joan** *grips her stomach in pain.* **Agnes** *tries to push past to get into* **Katherine**'s *room.*

Joan	I think it'll definitely bruise.
Agnes	If I am who you say I am –
	Shouldn't you be more careful?
Joan	Whatever spell you worked on the Lady –
	It'll wear off –
	And you'll be gone.
	I'll make sure of it.

Joan *bangs on* **Katherine**'s *door.*

Joan	My Lady?

Agnes *pushes past* **Joan** *and* **Anna**, *into the room.*

Mary	Did she do anything to you?
Joan	I hope not –
	But it's hard to tell with magic.
	She could be doing anything to us!
Anna	You don't think she's really casting spells on us –
	Do you?
Mary	She's always muttering.
	Makes me shiver.
Anna	But isn't she maybe –
	Just a bit odd?
Joan	No, Annie.
	She's a witch.
	I'm telling you.

Agnes *helps* **Katherine** *out of bed.*

Katherine	What's happening?
Agnes	Will only take a moment, My Lady,
	They need the sheets for cleaning –
	Blood takes a lot of work –
	So we find it best to –
Katherine	*Blood?*
Agnes	Yes.
	The blood –

Agnes *rips the sheet back, and there is no blood. A knock at the door.*

Joan	The Master will be home from the hunt soon.

Mary	You know how they like to do all the blood at once.
	Very lucky and all –
	Mine's just started.
Joan	And mine.
Anna	Really?

Agnes   Is this where you . . . lay with your husband?

Katherine   Yes.

Katherine *watches her, fiddling with a small looking glass.*

What's the matter?

Agnes   There is usually blood.

Unless you have –

Well –

I only say it, as it's what others will ask –

Katherine   Unless what?

Agnes   Unless you've been with another man.

Katherine   No!

Of course not!

No!

Anna	Both of you started bleeding?
	When?
Mary	This morning.
Joan	And I saw that Agnes left a horrible mess.
Mary	Oh I don't like it . . .
	Us all bleeding at the same time as a witch?
	That can't be good, can it?

Joan *knocks again.*

    Joan   Come on, Agnes –

    A good lady's maid doesn't leave the other servants waiting!

Katherine *calls out to the door –*

Katherine   Hold off!

    Joan   Sorry, My Lady.

Katherine   But *you know* –

    You know I haven't!

    I know you are a good person –

    And you must be thinking I am bad –

Agnes   *Good?*

    You think I'm good?

Katherine   Well of course you are –

    Look at you so shocked!

    But I promise I am too!

Elizabeth *arrives outside the door. She knocks.*

Katherine   I told you – Give me a moment!

    Elizabeth   Sorry Sister.

Katherine   Elizabeth! Sorry.

    A moment, please!

Katherine *looks at the sheets, looks at the door, then looks at* **Agnes**.

Katherine   There was no blood because nothing happened.

    Do you believe me?

    You have to believe me!

Agnes   What happened?

It's fine if you were scared –

Katherine   No.

I wasn't scared.

He didn't want me.

I was open and he didn't –

Is it that I'm not beautiful?

Am I ugly, Agnes?

Elizabeth   If we do not begin the day in an orderly
way

How are we to maintain order throughout?

Katherine   Let her in.

Let her think what she wants.

I'm not enough for this house.

I should've known that.

Agnes *looks at* **Katherine**. *She grabs the looking glass, smashes it,
and cuts the glass into her own hand, letting it bleed all over the
sheets.*

Agnes   Come in!

Elizabeth *enters.* **Agnes** *bundles up the sheets, and hands them
over.*

Elizabeth   They are wet?

Agnes   There was a visit this morning, Mistress.

Elizabeth   I will let you recover, sister.

Elizabeth *leaves,* **Anna**, **Joan** *and* **Mary** *walk away with the
sheets.*

Joan   One day –

One day with Agnes as lady's maid –

And our whole day is off –

Anna   Joan.

Joan   It's true!

Anna   I've not bled.

Joan   Oh. Don't worry, Annie –

It'll come.

Right?

Mary   Mine's always late.

Anna   It didn't come last month either.

I've prayed and I've prayed for it.

Joan   Well, we'll pray with you tonight –

Won't we?

Joan *and* **Mary** *put their arms around* **Anna**.

In her room, **Katherine** *takes a nightdress, and wraps it around* **Agnes**'s *hand*.

Katherine   As I said, old friends already.

Act II

Scene One

The **Devil** *plays the* **Physician**, *and inspects* **Katherine**'s *stomach.* **Elizabeth**, **Agnes**, **Joan** *and* **Anna** *are present. He steps aside with* **Elizabeth**.

> **Physician**   Still nothing, My Lady.
>
> **Elizabeth**   But it's been months!

Agnes *and* **Katherine** *talk.* **Agnes** *holds* **Katherine**'s *hand.*

> **Katherine**   She hates me –
>
> I feel it everyday –
>
> She hates me!
>
> Oh Agnes, what's wrong with me?
>
> **Physician**   I'm sorry, My Lady –
>
> But it would not be right if I did not ask about the rumours –
>
> **Elizabeth**   No, my good sir, I assure you that would be right.
>
> **Physician**   You know I am the most sceptical man for a hundred miles –
>
> But these rumours –
>
> Their persistence.
>
> It speaks to a.
>
> I hesitate to say it, My Lady –
>
> But they suggest a rot.
>
> **Elizabeth**   *A rot?*
>
> **Physician**   Yes, My Lady.

Joan *steps forward.* **Anna** *tries to stop her.*

Joan   Do you mean the witchcraft, Sir?

Elizabeth   Joan.

                  What have I told you about this?

Physician   The girl is right, My Lady –

                  I don't wish to tell any fireside tales –

                  But the witchcraft could be a symptom of –

                  Well –

                  Don't you feel it?

                  You only have to stand at your window and
                  look outside –

                  The people in this town are scared –

                  And the next –

                  And all the way to London –

                  Because the world –

                  It is wrong.

Elizabeth   The world may be wrong but this house is
                  right.

Physician   It only takes one rotten breath from one
                  blackened mouth –

                  And the mold will spread –

                  And it is this that could be affecting your
                  Lady –

                  And her chances –

Physician *turns to* **Agnes**.

Physician   You look after the Lady?

Agnes *nods.*

Physician   Have you seen any such wrongs in this house?

Agnes *shakes her head.*

Physician   The humours of the female body are very delicate –

And any pollution of this kind –

However small –

It could destroy any chance of life.

Agnes   It could?

Elizabeth   You're scaring the girl.

Physician   Good!

She needs to take it seriously.

Anna *turns to* **Joan** *and* **Mary**.

Anna   You think this might hurt my baby?

Mary   No Annie, you're fine!

Both of you.

Agnes   But what if –

What if some of this wrong –

This witchcraft –

What if it was done for the sake of good?

Physician   No good can come from evil.

And worse –

Any act of evil –

And evil spreads.

Joan   Did you hear that, Agnes?

Any act of evil –

And evil spreads?

Elizabeth	Are we finished, Doctor?
Physician	You pay me to be thorough, My Lady.

He leaves. **Elizabeth** *grabs* **Agnes**.

Elizabeth	Why didn't you warn me this could happen?
Agnes	It hasn't.
Elizabeth	You know if there's any problem with Katherine –
	I won't hesitate.
	She'll be out.
Agnes	It's not her!
Elizabeth	You realise the more people talk of witches –
	The more I will eventually need to hand one over –
Agnes	Talk to your brother.
	It's him you need.
	He won't touch her.
	Hasn't stopped him putting babies in other girls though.

Scene Two

Edward *talks to* **Mary** *and* **Joan**. **Elizabeth** *walks in as he is speaking*.

Edward	I must tell you though –
	I am starting to worry.
	I really am.
	I don't know what will make these traitors happy.

All of their demands are met –

And then more demands!

Where will it end?

Elizabeth   Edward.

Mary *and* **Joan** *leave.*

Edward   Still no beef, I see?

Elizabeth   Anna is pregnant.

Edward   How hard can it be?

Find cow

Kill cow

Eat cow

Elizabeth   Brother.

Edward   Oh Lizzie –

You know these girls you hire!

They do as they like –

And when it all ends up exactly as expected –

They blame me.

You'll figure something out.

Elizabeth   But I'm wondering why a servant girl has a baby inside her –

And not your wife?

Edward   The creation of life, sister.

Is God's work.

Who am I to say why God will grant one life and not another?

Elizabeth   So we can expect good news soon?

Yes?

Edward   You know I hate it when we fight.

Elizabeth   I'll expect good news then.

Edward   You had the wedding.

That's what you wanted.

The wedding.

The marriage.

The money.

Elizabeth   An heir.

An heir is what we need.

Edward   Sister.

Elizabeth   Don't you understand?

If we don't have one this house will go to Henry –

Or some other distant cousin –

Someone who doesn't even wear the name de Clare!

If anything were to happen to you now –

I'd be thrown out –

Edward   This is morbid.

Elizabeth   Where would I go, Edward?

Where?

Edward   Then you expect me to have the child of a trader?

Elizabeth   No. Of course.

Much better to have the child of a servant!

I see now.

Edward	The servant knows her place.
	Not this girl –
	Oh no –
	She thinks she's one of us –
	And that's supposed to be our legacy?
	Our family sat on the boat next to King William!
Elizabeth	Edward, if we want that again –
	We have to adapt –
Edward	Stop it, Lizzie –
	Stop it –
	You always do this –
	I've travelled all day and I'm tired
Elizabeth	Alright, brother, alright.

She walks over to him, and touches him.

	We won't fight
	How's your leg?
Edward	Sore. Those carriages are too cramped.
Elizabeth	We'll get a bigger one.

She gets on her knees and rubs his legs.

Edward	See – this is what I like.
	When you're kind to me
Elizabeth	I could sing for you?
Edward	I am not a child, Elizabeth.
Elizabeth	Of course.
	I know.

Edward   Do they have cows in town?

Elizabeth   Cows?

Edward   Yes, I wonder how they do it in town –

                Do they raise cows?

Elizabeth   How about I dress her for you?

Her hands move further up his leg.

                I promise you'll like her

Edward   I like this.

Elizabeth   I'll go to her room, and pick out a nightdress
                for her.

                It'll be like I've wrapped her up for you –

She is now rubbing his crotch.

Edward   Sister

Elizabeth   You don't have to think of her you know –

                You can think of anything you want –

Edward   And what should I think about?

Elizabeth   Anything

He moans.

                See?

                You can do that can't you?

                Now go see your wife.

He grabs her.

Edward   I don't want to.

Elizabeth   Go see Katherine.

He pushes her to the floor. They struggle.

                Go see her –

Edward   Lizzie.

A noise. They turn and **Katherine** *is watching them. When they see her, she runs away.*

Elizabeth   Fix it.

Edward   If she claims the house is hers –

                Then she should know what happens in it.

Elizabeth   Edward. Please.

                For once, do as you need.

Edward   You've never let me be a man, have you?

                I could have saved us you know –

                I could have done it –

                But if I'm just a stud to you –

                Here just to whisper encouragement in the ear of some –

                Some common girl –

                Then fine.

                I'll do it.

Scene Three

Edward *storms into* **Katherine**'*s room.*

Katherine   I didn't see anything.

Edward   I think you did.

Katherine   I don't mind.

                It is forgiven.

Edward   A lady doesn't forgive so easily.

                Are you a lady, Katherine?

Katherine   Am I?

Edward   If you have to ask –

She kisses him. He kisses her back. He pushes her away.

Katherine   What's wrong?

Edward   Nothing.

Katherine   Please.

You know what's wrong.

Edward   What do you want from me, Katherine?

Katherine   I want to be your wife.

Edward   We said vows.

Katherine   You know what I mean.

Edward   Then say it.

Katherine   You know what I mean!

Edward   Then say it.

Katherine   I want you to have sex with me.

Edward   Oh. That.

Katherine   Why don't you want me?

Edward   My love, please.

Katherine   I've done something wrong.

Edward   You haven't.

Katherine   Tell me what it is and I'll change it

Anything.

Edward   You would?

Katherine   Is it my hair?

Edward   No.

Katherine   My body?

Edward   No.

Katherine   My face?

Edward   You'll change your face?

Katherine   I'll try.

Edward   Then, no.

Katherine   You told me you have desires.

Edward   Yes.

Katherine   Tell me.

I'll fulfil them.

Edward   Anything?

Katherine   Anything.

Edward   Get on your hands and knees.

She kneels on her hands and knees.

Bark.

Katherine   Like a dog . . .?

Edward   Like a dog.

She barks like a dog.

Now lie flat.

She lies flat on her front.

Is that how a dog lies?

Belly up.

She lies on her back.

Pant.

She pants.

So this is what you think of me –

A man who wants to fuck his dog?

Katherine   No!

Edward   Clearly it is.

Katherine   I love you, Edward –

I love you.

Why can't you love me?

Edward   Enough.

Katherine   I can make you happy –

Love me –

Please will you love me –

Edward   Enough now, Katherine.

Katherine   But I love you!

Edward   That is *enough*.

Edward *finds* **Elizabeth**.

Edward   Lizzie?

Elizabeth!

Elizabeth   How did it go?

Edward   It didn't, Lizzie –

And it won't –

Elizabeth   Edward –

Edward   No, Lizzie.

For once –

Listen!

What you want –

This –

This mingling –

This is the real death of our house –

More than it falling down.

It won't do.

And I won't do it –

For as long as I live –

I will not bed that girl.

Scene Four

Upstairs, **Elizabeth** *and* **Agnes** *talk.*

Elizabeth   So can you do it?

Agnes   Remember, you need something in return.

In this case –

A life for a life.

Elizabeth *thinks.*

Elizabeth   There is another life in this house.

An unwanted life.

Agnes   Whose?

Elizabeth   You told me, Agnes –

Anna's baby.

Agnes   No.

Elizabeth   You could at least say no, Mistress.

Agnes   I will not take a life.

Elizabeth   Anna doesn't want that baby –

It'll ruin her –

She'll wake up one morning a little blood in her sheets –

Saved from a life of mockery and pain.

And Katherine –

Katherine will wake up –

All her dreams come true!

Agnes   Did you not hear the doctor?

No good comes from evil –

What kind of baby could come from this?

Not one Katherine deserves.

Agnes *starts to leave.*

Elizabeth   What do you want?

Agnes *stops.*

Agnes   I've told you.

To be good.

Elizabeth   Why?

Agnes   Because . . .

Elizabeth   Because why?

Agnes   Because I want to go to bed at night –

Safe.

Knowing that if God took me there and then –

He'd hold my hand as he did –

Happy to see me.

Elizabeth   Why then?

That's when you're scared, isn't it?

Because every night as you lie there in the dark –

You have thoughts, don't you?

Bad, ungodly thoughts –

Agnes   Doesn't everybody?

Elizabeth   Of course.

But theirs are small, aren't they?

Manageable –

Packed away again after a good meal or a quick roll in bed –

But ours.

No.

Ours are giant. Vivid and glittering –

Glowering at us everyday – aren't they?

Keeping us awake all night –

Thinking, plotting, dreaming –

Agnes   *I am good!*

Elizabeth   You're scared!

As I was –

Too much expectation –

Too much hope!

You need someone to tell you it's alright –

Stroke your hair and forgive you –

And I can do that, Agnes, I can.

It's alright.

It's all alright –

Humiliating – isn't it?

To want so much –

Believe you deserve just so much –

Agnes *nods.*

Elizabeth   But you do deserve it, Agnes –

You deserve it all!

So tell me –

What fills your head in the dark?

Agnes   Sometimes.

China.

I wonder how food tastes off it.

Elizabeth   We can walk to the kitchen right now.

Agnes   And silk –

I want to know how it feels on skin –

Not in dressing –

But in wearing –

Elizabeth   I'll have a dress made for you.

Agnes   And these walls.

Every curve in the wood. Every dent.

I want to feel them.

Know them.

And the paintings.

I want to feel those too.

And in the touching –

I want to know their stories –

Like I painted them myself –

Elizabeth   Just give me your hand –

Agnes   And I want to read every book in this house –

Elizabeth   They're yours –

Every one.

Agnes *pulls away from* **Elizabeth** *in her excitement.*

Agnes   No. Not *read* –

I want to *have read* every book in this house –

And to know which I like and which I don't
like –

And I want to know why I like what I like –

And why I don't like what I don't like –

Because I want –

I want to be –

Not the kind of person who wonders –

But the kind of person who knows –

The kind of person that is so –

So –

So beautiful that anyone who sees me feels
ugly –

So clever that anyone who hears me feels
stupid –

Elizabeth   And they are!

Agnes   So perfect –

That people –

Just in seeing me –

Finally see themselves for what they are –

Empty!

That they are nothing and I am everything!

Elizabeth And you are!

Agnes And I want –

Heaven –

I want to know that I deserve it –

Not everyone does –

But I do –

And one day I'll wake up and I'll know that it's time –

I'll walk right up to the door and I'll knock –

And they'll say come in –

We've been waiting!

This is it –

This perfect place –

Perfect enough –

And only for –

People as perfect as you –

And from there –

I'll look back –

At this place –

And these people –

And laugh.

Elizabeth Then let's build that place now –

Together.

Right here.

You said it yourself –

This house is like heaven –

Save this house –

And we can *earn* heaven together –

Agnes   We can?

Elizabeth   If you help me –

And you will, won't you?

Agnes   I.

Elizabeth   Agnes. You'll help?

Agnes   This is wrong.

Elizabeth   How could heaven be wrong?

Agnes   No.

These thoughts are the Devil –

Temptation pure and simple –

That doctor was right –

They're a pollution –

So please –

Stop.

You must stop.

Elizabeth   But Agnes, how can you not see it?

When he spoke of a rot –

He meant you.

That's what Joan feels –

I feel it –

And deep down –

Katherine feels it –

Doesn't she?

Agnes   No.

Elizabeth   And you do, don't you?

Deny it all you like –

But you feel it.

There's something wrong with you.

That's why you have to fight so hard.

You know.

You've always known.

Scene Five

Agnes *arrives in* **Katherine**'s *room.* **Katherine** *wails.*

Agnes   Mistress,

What's wrong?

Katherine   He doesn't want me.

Agnes   I'm sure that isn't true –

Katherine   Will you call me Katherine?

Agnes   Mistress –

Katherine   I have things to say that I can only say to a
                friend –

Agnes   I am your friend

Katherine   Then call me Katherine

Agnes   Katherine.

Katherine   It sounds childish but I believed only by
                marrying

I'd be a wife –

That all those tasks that my mother performed
so effortlessly –

That only by marrying –

I could do them too –

She tried to teach me but I never properly
listened –

Because I thought that

When it happened it would all come to me

That I would be right

But I'm not right –

Agnes   But you can learn!

Katherine   How?

I know it –

I will never be what they want –

Never.

I will never be the wife I thought I'd be.

Agnes   Don't say that –

I will do everything I can to help you –

Katherine   But you've already done that –

And here I am –

A failure.

They were right –

All my sisters!

I suppose they're all laughing at me now –

Oh Agnes.

I am so unhappy.

Do you think I'll ever be happy again?

Agnes   Katherine, stop it.

I can't hear you talk like this because.

Because.

–

If I am to call you Katherine –

To call myself your friend –

Then I must confess –

When that man asked me today if I had seen evil.

I lied.

I have seen evil.

Me.

It is me.

I am what's wrong with this house.

I am what's causing all this for you.

Katherine   No.

I don't believe it.

Agnes   Ask anyone and they will tell you –

Agnes is a witch!

But I swear it, Katherine –

I was not –

I never fit that name –

Everyday I fought against it.

Katherine   Of course you did!

Agnes	But then I stepped into this house –
	And I did do evil –
	And I did it for the Lady Elizabeth.
Katherine	No.
Agnes	Yes.
Katherine	I knew it.
Agnes	You did?
Katherine	No.
	Not really –
	But I have seen her –
	Doing things I cannot say with my husband and –
	Do you think she did a spell on him –
	To make him hate me?
	Yes!
	That's it!
	You have to expose her.
	Oh Agnes, you have to.
	You have to!
Agnes	But.
	I would have to expose myself.
Katherine	Of course.
	Yes.
	We don't want you to do that.
	But.
	There must be another way.

	What about –
	Who are those men Joan spoke of –
	They travel and find witches?
Agnes	A Witchfinder?
Katherine	Yes, how silly of me.
	Could we call on one of those?
	Have them come here?
Agnes	They'd find me.
Katherine	Of course they wouldn't.
	You haven't done anything!
	This Witchfinder –
	Whoever he is.
	And he'll see evil in her –
	Just as you have –
	Just as I have –
	And not in you –
	Because you're good, aren't you?
	What evil person confesses?
	No, no –
	He'll mark her a witch –
	And he'll send her away!
	And then, Agnes –
	Oh Agnes –
	Think on it –
	I'll have this whole house to myself!

	My whole husband –
	All mine.
Agnes	Maybe it is time.
	Finally time . . .
Katherine	Then you'll call him?
Agnes	I'll call him.
	It's time.
	It's the only way.

Act III

Scene One

The **Devil** *plays the* **Witchfinder**. **Katherine**, **Agnes**, **Joan**, **Mary** *and* **Anna** *are in attendance. He inspects* **Mary**. *He finds a mark on her leg, and pokes it. She winces.*

Mary   Please Sir –

                      I've always had that –

Agnes *speaks to* **Katherine**.

          Katherine   Where is my sister?

                              You said she was coming?

          Agnes   She is.

Mary   Mistress!

                      Please.

          Agnes   It's not Mary.

                              Stop him.

          Anna   Do you think this will hurt my baby?

          Joan   Don't worry, Annie.

                              I'll end this.

Katherine *addresses the* **Witchfinder**.

Katherine   Sorry –

                      Are these methods really necessary?

Witchfinder You can't hold back in the face of the Devil.

Katherine   But –

                      Isn't the girl in pain?

He stops.

Witchfinder My Lady.

I'm sorry.

I have been charged with being overzealous before.

And I do wish to fight these accusations –

So, if you wish me to stop.

I will stop.

Katherine Good.

Then stop searching this girl –

And look where I tell you.

Witchfinder You misunderstand, My Lady –

If I stop, I leave.

If I continue –

I continue with my method.

With no interference.

Katherine But.

But I asked you here . . .

Witchfinder And why did you?

Is it because you –

Like so many others –

Find yourself thwarted in all you do?

Not just from outside –

But on the inside as well –

You wake up in the morning –

Not with cheer –

But with a hardness in your gut –

And as you try to share it with those around you –

A cold air keeps them always just at a distance?

That is evil.

You've felt it –

Haven't you?

Katherine *nods.*

Witchfinder And the rest of you?

He looks at the servants, they nod. He turns back to **Katherine***.*

Witchfinder So will you let me find it?

Katherine Yes. Look anywhere.

He gestures for the next servant. **Joan***,* **Anna** *and* **Agnes** *jostle.*

Joan There's no need to investigate all of us –

When we all know the one person who it is –

Witchfinder You do?

Joan Yes.

Don't we?

Mary I.

I think so . . .

Elizabeth *walks in.*

Elizabeth What is this?

Witchfinder I have been tasked with finding evil.

Elizabeth But who has tasked you?

Katherine I.

I felt it was time to put an end to these rumours –

Elizabeth   How wise.

Aren't I lucky to have you?

And may I ask –

Have you found any evil?

Witchfinder Not yet, My Lady –

Elizabeth   And what are you looking for?

Witchfinder I will know it when I see it.

Elizabeth   That seems rather arduous –

Why not tell me the signs and maybe I can help?

Witchfinder I don't think so.

Elizabeth   But I know this house better than anyone.

Witchfinder Forgive me –

But a moment ago –

You didn't know that I had been called –

And if I can sneak in unannounced –

Then evil certainly can.

In any cut on the hand –

Or on the wrist?

And I believe we were on our way to our first allegation.

Weren't we?

Joan   Well.

I.

Elizabeth   *Joan?*

Witchfinder Speak.

God is your master here –

	Your mistress understands that –
	Doesn't she?

Joan *hesitates, and then steps forward, and points at* **Agnes**.

Joan	It's her, Sir –
	I've heard her –
	Muttering before she goes to sleep –
	And she.
	She went from shovelling mud –
	To a lady's maid –
	And how do you explain that?
Witchfinder	Is this true?
Mary	I've heard rumours.
Anna	So have I.

He turns to **Katherine**.

Witchfinder	And have you heard anything, My Lady?
Katherine	I.
	Well.
Witchfinder	Agnes, what do you have to say?
Agnes	I.
Witchfinder	Do you want me to search you?
Agnes	You.
	You don't need to.
	It's true.
Joan	See!
Agnes	For ever, people have pointed at me and said evil –
	But I fought it –

I did –

I fought and fought –

Everyday –

Until –

Until I stepped into this house

And then.

Then.

Witchfinder Then you did magic?

Agnes *nods.*

Witchfinder What magic?

Agnes For her.

I did it for her.

Witchfinder For the lady of the house?

Agnes Yes.

A spell.

With blood.

Her blood.

Joan She's lying.

It wasn't –

It was just for her.

Witchfinder You are quiet, My Lady –

Elizabeth And why should I speak?

Witchfinder To beg your place beside God.

Elizabeth God knows I stand by his side.

Witchfinder But do I?

Elizabeth   And who are you?

Witchfinder   The man who stands between this house and
salvation –

Elizabeth   I believe that's blasphemy.

Witchfinder   Only the guilty throw accusations when
accused.

Elizabeth   Mary. Fetch my brother.

Mary *leaves*.

Witchfinder   You will not even attempt a defence?

Elizabeth   And why should I?

The girl is a servant angry at a scolding.

Witchfinder   I see.

The girl is a servant . . .

But you are *a lady*?

Elizabeth   Yes.

A lady.

Witchfinder   Do you forget who Jesus chose to stand by his
side?

Not ladies.

You think the Devil only travels through mud?

He likes his perfume as much as you do –

And if he's been fraternising here –

I wouldn't be surprised.

Elizabeth   You are not a holy man –

You are a peddler of tricks and tales –

I know your kind –

                Like those men fighting the King –

                Big, empty words –

                Heard in the moment –

                Forgotten the next.

                You'll see.

Edward   But do you, My Lady?

                We are everywhere –

                In your towns –

                On your land –

                Amongst your staff –

                Breeding faster and faster –

Edward *comes in.*

Edward   Who is this?

Elizabeth   He is our salvation, brother.

Witchfinder Did you know it, Sir –

                Your sister –

                She is a witch?

Edward *hits him.*

Edward   You're one of them, aren't you?

                They're sending them here now, are they?

                The traitors?

                I'll have you flogged –

                And chained up on the street –

                As the lunatic you are.

Witchfinder Do as you like, Sir –

                But remember –

People will hear about today –

And what was said.

They won't like it.

And they will come for you.

England is not what it was –

All over men are choosing the proper faith –

Not one of gold, and rubies and long, Latin words –

But one that states that in the eyes of God –

All are dirt on the ground.

You mask that –

Try and float above –

But they will knock you down.

And soon.

Edward *drags him from the room.* **Elizabeth** *turns to* **Joan** *and slaps her in the face.*

Elizabeth   Leave us.

Joan, **Mary** *and* **Anna** *run away.* **Elizabeth** *is silent. She thinks.*

Katherine   I.

I had to.

There were rumours and.

And.

Elizabeth   I am done.

It is over.

What I did I only ever did for this house –

This was once a great house –

> A *great* house –
>
> And I only wanted to restore that –
>
> For you, Katherine –

She takes **Katherine**'s *hands.*

Elizabeth   I only wanted you to have the house you deserved –

You can forgive me –

Can't you?

And we can be sisters as sisters should be?

Katherine *nods.*

Elizabeth   And Agnes.

I am sorry to put you in such a position.

Truly.

You were right.

I did evil.

And I made you do evil.

It needed to stop.

You can forgive me?

Agnes *nods.* **Elizabeth** *turns to* **Katherine**.

Elizabeth   Then I suppose you're happy for the baby to be born?

Katherine   –

What baby?

Elizabeth   I see Agnes has been shielding you –

From the full reach of my evil.

Because I asked Agnes to prevent the birth of a
baby –

But she refused –

Like the good girl she is.

Katherine   Whose baby?

Elizabeth   Anna's.

Katherine   But why would you . . .?

Elizabeth   Very sweet girl.

And I was going to take away her baby.

Thank the Lord for Agnes!

Katherine   Who was the father?

Elizabeth   No, no, sister –

I've learned the error of my ways.

We won't dwell –

But deal with the child when God brings it
forth.

Katherine *looks at* **Agnes**, *who looks away.*

Katherine   Who was the father?

Agnes   You don't –

Katherine   Tell me.

Agnes   *Please.*

Katherine   Who was the father?

Agnes   Your husband.

A pause.

Katherine   My husband?

Elizabeth   This is what I wished to spare you.

But now we shall all live together, happily –

Won't we?

You. Edward. And Anna's baby.

There will be talk of course.

You know how people are –

Look at the shape of that boy's brow?

What a noble brow it is.

It must mean there is nobility somewhere within!

But you'll learn to live with it –

Won't you?

Though it may be difficult.

Especially with your own impediments in that area –

Agnes *takes* **Katherine**'*s arm.*

Agnes   You should lie down.

But **Katherine** *doesn't move.*

Elizabeth   But now that we've all sworn to be good –

Maybe my brother will finally do his duty –

And you'll have a child of your own.

But that brings with it a different kind of difficulty, doesn't it?

Because people will compare, won't they?

Aren't they similar?

Those two boys?

But which one is taller?

Faster? The better hunter?

Sadly I think I know which it will be.

Remember.

Servant stock is strong.

Anna might give birth to a boy with wide square shoulders –

And long, firm legs.

Perfect for hunting.

And my brother would like that wouldn't he?

The great hunter.

But I'm sure you'll bear it well, sister –

Sat down at dinner –

Two deer in front of you –

One small –

Killed in a struggle –

When it was already wounded –

By the weak hand of your fragile son –

Born from the tepid lovemaking that comes of duty –

And the other –

Spread across the whole table –

Enough for an army –

Killed with a single arrow to the centre of the heart –

By the steady hand of the servant child –

Born with the potency only illicit carnality can bring

Which plate will Edward choose?

I think you know –

Don't you?

Because why would anyone choose anything else?

Agnes *turns to* **Katherine**.

Agnes   You need to lie down.

Elizabeth   Yes –

Lie down.

It's a shock sister –

But remember –

Wives have borne worse.

Agnes *pulls* **Katherine** *away*.

Scene Two

Katherine *flops onto her bed, and cries*.

Katherine   Those girls, Agnes –

Those girls –

I hate them all –

Oh Agnes, am I so much uglier than those girls?

Agnes   Katherine, no.

Katherine   My nose is crooked and my cheeks are thin.

Agnes   Your nose is straight and your cheeks are plump

Katherine   Not like Anna.

Her cheeks are fat.

How is it a servant has such fat cheeks?

And when we don't even have any beef.

Go fetch Joan.

I'll tell her.

Stop feeding them.

He will have anyone.

Anyone but me.

I hate it here I hate it here I hate it here.

Agnes   Stop it.

You are beautiful.

You are kind.

Katherine   You knew. Didn't you?

Agnes   And I knew how much it would hurt you.

Katherine   Why does everyone think I'm a child!

Do you think I'm a child?

Agnes   No!

Katherine   Tell me what you know about Anna.

She tempted him, didn't she?

Agnes   She's not the only one.

Katherine   Well.

They all tempted him.

Agnes   And she won't be last.

Katherine   Agnes!

Agnes   Don't you see?

This gives you freedom!

Katherine	Freedom?
Agnes	You see who he is now –
	What this house is!
	You could leave –
Katherine	Leave?
Agnes	Yes.
Katherine	But.
Agnes	You could go back to your family.
Katherine	And have them laugh at me.
	Kitty has another failure.
Agnes	Well then live alone.
Katherine	*Alone?*
Agnes	I know it sounds hard –
	But it only takes imagination.
	Mistress Elizabeth is not married –
	And she has other friends who aren't.
	Who live full lives
	Either away from their husbands –
	Or with no husband at all.
	You can live that way.
Katherine	I can't.
Agnes	You can!
	I'll be there to look after you.
Katherine	You will?
Agnes	Of course.

Katherine	I can't.
Agnes	You can change this –
Katherine	No.
	There are things I will have to be used to.
	I will have to adjust –
	Accept.
	But I am sure most wives accept this.
Agnes	But you don't have to –
Katherine	I do not expect you to understand for you are a servant girl.
	And I should not have to explain it to you
	For again
	You are a servant girl.
	But I was raised to marry a man of nobility.
	And now I have.
	This is what grown wives must bear.
	And I will bear it.
Agnes	Katherine –
Katherine	You will do as my sister has asked.
	And you will get rid of that girl's baby.
Agnes	*Katherine –*
Katherine	And you will call me Mistress
Agnes	Then I won't, Mistress.
Katherine	You will do it.
	You will do it.
	You will do it.

Agnes   He doesn't love you.

He'll never love you.

A knock at the door, and a voice from outside – **Edward***'s.*

Edward   My love.

Are you there?

Katherine *is suddenly overcome with tears and hurt. She weeps into her pillow.*

Agnes   Tell him to leave.

Katherine *looks at* **Agnes***. With hate. With rage. And an idea strikes her. She calls out to the door.*

Katherine   Sorry my love,

A moment.

Katherine *picks up her own night dress. She hands it to* **Agnes***.*

Katherine   Put it on.

Agnes   But Katherine –

Katherine   I am your *mistress*.

You do as *I say*.

Agnes *dresses in* **Katherine***'s clothes.* **Katherine** *calls to* **Edward***.*

Katherine   My love, are you still there?

Katherine *hides behind a screen.* **Edward** *enters.*

Edward   How could you allow an enemy into our walls –

This house can withstand an army –

But not you?!

He sees **Agnes***.*

Edward   What have we here?

Agnes   Mistress?

Agnes *looks at* **Katherine***'s hiding place.* **Edward** *follows her gaze and sees* **Katherine***.*

Edward   A game –

                  Is it?

He moves onto the bed. **Agnes** *gets off it.*

Edward   Won't you sit with me?

Agnes   *Mistress?*

Edward   What is this Mistress?

                  My wife calls no one Mistress.

Agnes   She doesn't?

Edward   My wife knows no Mistress but her own mind.

                  What would make you sit back on the bed?

Agnes   If you weren't on it, Sir.

Edward   Sir?

                  I am your husband.

                  Call me Edward.

Agnes   Then Edward.

                  Stand over there.

Edward   Where?

Agnes   There.

Edward *gets up, and walks to the other side of the room.*

Edward   Anything for the lady.

Agnes   I'm a lady?

Edward   I am a lord.

                  My wife is a lady.

Agnes   And what does a lady do?

Edward	Anything she wants.
Agnes	Anything?
Edward	Yes. I'm waiting.
Agnes	For what?
Edward	My next command.
Agnes	Get on the floor.

> On your hands and knees.
>
> –
>
> Like a dog.

He gets onto his hands and knees.

Edward	Anything for the lady.
Agnes	That's not how a dog speaks –

> Is it?

He barks.

> Louder.

He barks louder.

> Don't you want all your friends to hear you in the kennels?

He howls.

> Good boy.

He starts to crawl towards the bed, and starts to climb onto the bed. She slaps his hand, and pushes him off.

> Dogs are not allowed on the bed –
>
> Are they?

He sits on the floor at her feet and howls. She takes his slapped hand in hers, and kisses it.

> What would you do to get on this bed?

Edward   Anything.

Agnes   Then prove it.

Scene Three

Katherine *cries and finds* **Elizabeth**.

Katherine   She's the witch!

She's the witch –

Agnes.

I want her gone.

Elizabeth   Are you sure?

Katherine   You told me!

Elizabeth   This is a serious accusation, sister –

I need to be sure.

What's she done?

Katherine   She –

She –

I just know it!

I need her gone.

Elizabeth   I can do that –

Of course –

But in return I will need you to do as I say.

Katherine   Anything.

Elizabeth   No more rebellions –

No more tantrums –

You will be a lady in name –

And in name only –

This is my house –

And you will treat it as such.

Katherine *nods.*

Elizabeth   Come with me.

Scene Four

Back in the bedroom, **Agnes** *cleans in her own clothes.* **Elizabeth** *and* **Katherine** *enter.*

Elizabeth   Agnes.

Come with me.

Agnes *continues to clean.*

Elizabeth   Leave that.

Just follow.

Agnes *looks at them.*

Agnes   Where?

Elizabeth   That man will be talking about us to anyone who'll listen –

And something must be done.

Agnes   What will happen to me?

Elizabeth   My brother will alert the authorities in the morning –

You'll be locked up.

There will be a trial.

They will find you guilty –

And then you'll hang.

Agnes   I won't go alone.

I'll tell them it was you.

Elizabeth   These men won't be like the Witchfinder.

They're local people.

They know me –

And more importantly –

They know you.

Agnes *rushes to* **Katherine**.

Agnes   Whatever she's told you is a lie –

I confessed –

Remember?

I am good –

It is all her.

All her.

Katherine *looks away.*

Elizabeth   Katherine came to me, Agnes.

I didn't say anything.

Elizabeth *tries to grab her, but* **Agnes** *pulls away.* **Agnes** *gets down on her knees in front of* **Katherine**.

Agnes   I'm sorry –

I'm sorry!

I only did as you asked –

But still –

I will do all I can to make you happy –

Anything!

Everything!

Please!

Old friends?

Remember? Old friends?

Katherine *looks away.*

Elizabeth   It's time.

Elizabeth *tries to grab her again,* **Agnes** *pushes her away.*

Agnes   I confessed –

For you –

Risked my life for your happiness –

And now you –

Katherine –

Sweet Katherine –

You would see me hang?

–

Look at me, Katherine!

At least look.

Katherine   It is, Mistress.

Agnes   No it isn't.

It's my blood on your sheets, *Katherine* –

I may be a woman –

But you're still a girl.

Katherine   You're not a woman, you're a witch!

Agnes   No.

Katherine   Yes!

You tempted me!

	You tempted all of us!
	You're evil!
Agnes	If you call me evil –
	I will be evil –
	And *Katherine* –
	You won't like it.
Katherine	It is *Mistress!*
	Mistress! Mistress! Mistress!

Agnes *laughs at her, and turns to* **Elizabeth**.

Agnes	And so this is who you choose?
	This –
	The woman who'll make all those –
	Great glittering dreams of yours, true?
	Or shall I call them what they'll be now?
	Regrets –
	The lost dreams of a woman who everyone remembers –
	But nobody knows.
Elizabeth	I'll manage.
Agnes	No.
	You won't.
	Not without me.

Elizabeth *tries to grab* **Agnes**, *but* **Agnes** *pushes her off, and runs away.*

| **Elizabeth** | Agnes! |

Scene Five

Agnes *finds somewhere private.*

Agnes   Speak to me –

                   You who everyone says has spoken to me my
                   whole life –

                   You who, according to all, are my closest
                   companion –

                   Speak!

The **Devil** *appears.* **Agnes** *screams.*

The Devil   Finally!

Agnes   So I am yours?

The Devil   If you want to be –

Agnes   I do.

                   I want it all.

                   I want everything.

                   Every bad thought –

                   Every evil.

                   I want them now.

The Devil   I'm glad!

                   Though –

                   I don't know how much of that I can give that
                   to you.

Agnes   My whole life I lived in denial of what you
                   offered –

                   Because I believed the price was too great –

                   But I always believed the rewards were great
                   also –

	And now I call on you –

And now I call on you –

Finally call on you –

Ready to pay that price –

And you say no?

The Devil   Who are you?

Agnes   I'm Agnes.

The Devil   And what is she?

Agnes   A.

A lady's maid.

The Devil   And wasn't she a stable girl?

And isn't she also a witch?

Or just the daughter of one?

Is she good like *she* says?

Or evil like *everyone else* says?

Agnes   Aren't you supposed to be the one to tell me?

The Devil   No, Agnes –

You tell me.

Because you can be any one of those –

Or none of them –

Don't you see?

You can be anything you want to be –

Agnes   But –

How?

The Devil   Oh come on, Agnes –

You're so close.

As you said –

It's your blood on the sheets . . .

Agnes   It is – isn't it?

The Devil   But I have to ask –

You know what it'll cost –

Don't you?

Agnes   Hell?

The Devil   It's as bad as you think –

Worse.

No words could ever do it justice.

Agnes   I'm ready.

Scene Six

Downstairs, **Joan** *comes back into bed to see* **Anna** *and* **Mary**.

Joan   She confessed!

Anna   Oh stop it –

Joan   Anna.

You were there!

You saw it!

Mary   Smart move of her to blame the lady –

That will get all the talk stopped.

Joan   Exactly!

But then she notices **Anna** *wincing.*

Joan   You're in pain?

I'll sleep with Mary tonight –

You need the space.

Anna   I need the warmth more . . .

Joan *lies in bed next to her.*

Joan   See! We'll all fit in here.

              You, me and little John.

Anna   You know, Joanie –

              I think he'll be blonde.

Scene Seven

Agnes *sits having her portrait painted by an* **Artist**, *played by the* **Devil**. *She wears* **Katherine**'s *clothes, and they fit her better than they ever fit* **Katherine**.

Artist   A very fine collection you have here, My Lady

Agnes   Oh yes, my sister, Elizabeth, is a very fine
              collector . . .

Agnes *looks out to the audience – addresses us directly . . .*

              Boo!

And she laughs.

Interval.

Act IV

Scene One

Agnes *sits for the* **Artist** *(played by the* **Devil***) in* **Katherine***'s clothes.*

Artist	A very fine collection you have here, My Lady.
Agnes	Oh yes, my sister, Elizabeth, is a very fine collector . . .
Artist	Oh I know.
	And a very fine subject as well . . .
Agnes	Is this *gossip?*
Artist	Nothing that isn't well known.
Agnes	Then you must share.
Artist	There is a portrait of her in Conneth House
	From the lady's days in Court.
	It was commissioned by Lord Astley –
	A former admirer.
Agnes	Oh *really?*
Artist	The man wrote her letters enough to fill the Bible.
	And as you can imagine –
	Wives don't like that kind of thing.
Agnes	Oh *dear.*
Artist	So the painting was hung in the laundry.
	Where everything goes that is dirty.
Agnes	My sister won't like that.

Artist	It's led to a great tradition of art appreciators –
	Spilling drinks on themselves at Lady Astley's parties –
	So they might sneak into the laundry and glimpse the painting –
Agnes	You said you've seen it yourself?
Artist	And I lost a great shirt for the privilege.
Agnes	Well, I'm sure I have a few dresses I can spare.
Artist	On the subject of gossip . . .
	I read a very curious pamphlet . . .
	Suggesting there were witches in this house –
Agnes	Those pamphleteers will say anything to discredit my husband.
Artist	Of course, My Lady –
	Of course.
	I am sorry.
	I shouldn't read those rags –
	But I must say I prefer those quaint tales of village evil –
	To those about stripping the King of his power.
Agnes	Is that possible?
Artist	Well exactly!
Agnes	And where do these pamphleteers suggest the power goes?
Artist	Parliament, if you can believe it.
	Some go even further –
	They talk of power –

In the hands of the people!

They want us all equals –

Levelled out –

Peasant, priest and pomp alike!

Agnes   I take it you don't like this?

Artist   My, my –

Lady de Clare –

Do I find myself in the presence of a radical?

Agnes   Tell me.

Why shouldn't you take a fancy down the lane –

Pick up a peg seller –

And paint her in my seat?

Artist   You *are* a radical.

Agnes   As you're not answering, I'll assume you're one yourself.

Artist   I have spent my whole life –

In houses like this –

And what I have always found is true refinement –

Simply not present anywhere else.

Because the simple fact is –

God places us in our mother's wombs –

He knows where we shall start out and where we shall end up

It is his plan.

God gave me the hands of a painter –

And you, My Lady –

God has given the ample beauty and brilliance to tackle –

Those secret tasks of ladies.

Agnes   He has?

Artist   Oh yes, My Lady –

Just look at you!

Elizabeth *walks in.*

Elizabeth How goes the painting?

Artist   Very well, My Lady!

Elizabeth *looks at the painting.*

Artist   Though it has been hard work –

For your charming sister has been very distracting!

Then she looks at **Agnes**.

Agnes   Then you should not tell such good stories!

Sister –

I have been hearing all about Sir Astley's dedication to you.

I think when we are next in London

We shall have to invite ourselves over –

And sneak in to see the painting!

Elizabeth No.

No no no no no.

Agnes   I've not upset you now?

I promise – I only want to admire you!

Elizabeth *turns to the* **Artist** –

Elizabeth	Who is the woman that sits for you?
Artist	My Lady –
Elizabeth	Humour me.
Artist	Alright.
	Well. The lady who has been such distraction –
	Only at the cost of her own likeness –
	Leading me to believe she does not want me to catch it –
Agnes	Maybe I worry I am not a great subject
	For such a great artist!
Artist	Oh you are!
	Lady – the finest!
Elizabeth	*Who is it?*
Artist	Your sister
	The Lady de Clare . . .
Elizabeth	Mary.
	Mary.
	MARY.

Mary *enters the room.*

Mary	Yes, My Lady.
Elizabeth	Who is this?

Mary *looks at* **Agnes**. *Looks at* **Elizabeth**, *confused.*

Mary	Mistress?
Agnes	Is everything alright, sister?
Elizabeth	Who is it?

Mary   The Lady, Mistress.

Elizabeth   *Who?*

Mary   The Lady de Clare . . .

Agnes *walks over to her* . . .

Agnes   Elizabeth –

Elizabeth *slaps her across the face and turns to* **Mary** *and the* **Artist**.

Elizabeth   Leave us.

They leave.

Agnes   The artist seems very happy.

                  He is very talented –

                  Can you imagine?

                  Picking up a brush and some colourful pastes –

                  And creating the world in miniature?

Elizabeth   Get changed now.

Agnes   Sister –

Elizabeth   Don't.

                  You will change

                  Now.

Agnes   But what will you say to the artist?

Elizabeth   I will get Katherine.

Agnes   But I am Katherine.

Elizabeth   You are a stable girl.

                  A witch!

                  You will change now.

                  Into rags.

                  And go back down the road you came from.

Agnes   The Lady de Clare in rags for her inaugural
                   portrait . . .

                   It's modest.

                   Marking that wherever we come from –

                   We all end up in the same dirt.

                   A bold choice, sister.

                   But I prefer the classic, don't you?

Elizabeth   One last chance.

                   Change.

Agnes   No.

She shouts to the door.

                   Hello!

                   We are well!

The **Artist** *returns.*

Agnes   My sister has headaches, I am sorry.

                   Shall we continue?

Artist   Oh, I understand.

                   I find air helps.

Agnes *sits back down, and the* **Artist** *continues.*

Elizabeth   Stop.

The **Artist** *stops.*

Elizabeth   You will stop with the painting.

                   And you will leave.

Artist   My Lady –

Agnes   Air, sister.

                   As the good man has said.

She turns to the **Artist**.

Agnes I am so sorry.

The trials you read of in the pamphlet –

They have left their mark.

Artist As they would.

The **Artist** *continues.*

Elizabeth I said stop!

Agnes Sister –

Why don't you explain to us –

Exactly why it is you want this talented man to stop his work –

And maybe we can help?

Elizabeth *freezes. She knows she can't say.*

Elizabeth This is my house.

I do not have to explain anything.

Agnes No, sister.

This is *my* house.

And I would like to continue –

So we will continue.

The **Artist** *continues.*

Elizabeth This is not my sister!

She is an imposter!

Agnes *and the* **Artist** *look at each other.*

Elizabeth A witch!

Agnes *starts to laugh.*

Agnes I shouldn't.

It's too cruel –

But since all those rumours started –

She really does say the maddest things.

And what else am I to do?

Artist   You are a saint, My Lady.

Agnes   No, no.

I just do as any sister would.

Mary?

Mary *enters.*

Agnes   Will you escort the Lady on a walk?

And don't forget her coat, now.

Mary *nods, and tries to take* **Elizabeth***'s arm,* **Elizabeth** *pushes her away, and walks outside,* **Mary** *follows.*

Agnes   The head of woman.

Such a sensitive little creature, isn't it?

Artist   From a man who has spent his life trying to capture it,

It is, My Lady, oh, it is.

Agnes *now turns out to us, the audience.*

Agnes   Is this man right?

Are we born a lady?

I think not.

You see it's not hard to be a lady.

When people hear the title –

They expect to see a lady –

As long as you behave like one –

Then a lady you are.

Do you see a lady?

Maybe you don't know that means anymore.

Maybe you're beyond everything that it means to be a lady –

A lady to you is strange, quaint –

Empty?

And what about this house?

Once when I looked at it, I saw –

A tall stack of bricks –

Not much more.

But now it's.

Now it could be –

Joan?

Joan *rushes into the room.*

Joan	Yes, My Lady –
Agnes	My sister has just had a baby –
Joan	Congratulations, Mistress.
Agnes	Thank you, Joan –
	She sent me this medicine –
	It's meant to help in the late months –
	I thought maybe there was someone in the house –
	Someone who might benefit?

Agnes *hands* **Joan** *a bottle.*

Joan	Oh Mistress –
	This is too kind!

Don't you want to save it –

For when you might need it yourself?

Agnes   She sent plenty – too much!

Please. Take it.

Scene Two

Katherine   Sister –

I know you will not think it –

Elizabeth *attacks her.*

Elizabeth *finds* **Katherine**.

Elizabeth   How could you let this happen?

How could you let her?

Katherine   I didn't! I didn't!

Elizabeth   You did!

She is a servant!

A stable girl!

And you spoke to her –

You made her your friend –

Your accomplice –

Let her speak your given name and now she wears it!

How did it happen?

How has she done this?

Katherine   I don't know!

I don't know!

Elizabeth   You do know!

Katherine	She lay with my husband –
	She seduced him –
Elizabeth	Every woman in the house has fucked my brother!
	Do they walk around calling themselves ladies?
Katherine	She wore my nightdress . . .
Elizabeth	And how did she get into your nightdress?
Katherine	I put it on her.
Elizabeth	You put that filthy girl in your clothes?
Katherine	I needed to see!
	He wouldn't touch me –
	I had to see!
Elizabeth	You should have lain in bed and pretended to be asleep –
	Let him do what he wanted –
	Then we'd have an heir –
	But like a child you had to be loved, didn't you?
	Are you a baby, Katherine?
	A little baby crying out for mummy and daddy?
	Because I see breasts, Katherine –
	I see the body of a woman –
	Do you have hair on your cunt, Katherine?
	Does it bleed every month?
	Well?
	Does it?

Katherine   Yes!

Elizabeth   Then you are a woman and you will act like one.

Katherine   I'm sorry –

Mistress – I'm sorry –

Elizabeth   Mistress!

I'm your sister!

Your junior!

You are the lady of the house!

You could order me to scrub the floor before you

As you walk if you wished –

And yet you lie on the floor –

Cry and call me Mistress!

Katherine   I'm sorry! I'm sorry!

Elizabeth   No.

This is my fault.

I never gave you the tools to defend yourself.

But I will teach you now.

I will make you earn it.

Katherine   So I will be me again?

Elizabeth   Did you think I'd let that witch remain?

You'll be back.

When my brother returns I will tell him everything –

And then –

We will strip her.

We will beat her

And then we will tell everyone who she is

And we will hang her.

Scene Three

Downstairs, **Joan** *finds* **Anna** –

Joan   I have a present for you!

She hands **Anna** *the vial* –

Joan   Meant to be good in the later months.

Anna   Who's it from?

Joan   The Lady Katherine –

Very kind of her –

Don't you think?

Anna   Very, very kind!

And look at the bottle!

So beautiful!

You know when the baby is born –

I think I shall wear this around my neck –

For luck, you know?

She drinks it.

Scene Four

Agnes *and* **Edward** *now sit at the dinner table, when* **Elizabeth** *walks in.*

Elizabeth   Brother –

I need to speak with you.

Edward	In a moment, sit down.
Elizabeth	I promise, brother –
	It is important.
Edward	Sister.
	I have travelled all day.
	And I have news.
	Sit down.
Elizabeth	Edward.
	I demand that you get up and speak to me!
Edward	The King has fled London.
	The King –
	Himself –
	Is exiled from the capital of the country he is King of.
	What could you possibly have to say?

Elizabeth *sits down.*

Elizabeth	When did it happen?
Edward	I don't know.
	A few days ago?
	No one told me!
Elizabeth	Everyone has a lot on their minds, I suppose.
Edward	But still –

Joan *and the other servants appear at the door carrying dinner plates.* **Agnes** *holds up a hand and asks her to wait, she stands up and addresses the table.*

Agnes	I have organised a surprise for this evening –

And maybe that is just what we need.

Please cover your eyes.

Edward   I won't do anything of the sort.

Agnes   Well then, I shall do it for you.

She holds her hands over **Edward**'s *eyes.*

Elizabeth   You will sit back down and wait for your food
in silence.

Agnes   Sister, relax!

Agnes *signals to* **Joan** *who brings out their food alongside*
Katherine, **Mary** *and* **Anna**, *who stumbles with the food, looking
ill.* **Agnes** *takes her hands away from* **Edward**'s *eyes.*

Agnes   Surprise!

Edward *looks down and is amazed.*

Edward   Is it?

Agnes   Red and bloody as you like it.

In the background, **Joan** *sees* **Anna** *doesn't look well . . .*

    Joan   Are you alright?

    Anna   I'm fine –

Baby's hungry is all.

Edward   Beef. Beef!

I can't believe it.

How did you do this?

Agnes   You wouldn't have me give away all my secrets,

Now would you?

Edward *pulls her onto his lap, and kisses her.*

Edward   Oh my love! My love!

Agnes *tries to stand up, but* **Edward** *pulls her back down.*

Edward   Oh no, no, no –

You'll never leave my sight –

You beautiful, miraculous little creature!

I hope every King-fearing man in this country –

Has a good slab of beef for dinner this evening –

A good, firm, red bullet in everyone's bellies –

He kisses **Agnes**, *and begins to eat with glee.* **Katherine** *watches, devastated.*

In the background, **Mary** *has now noticed* **Anna.**

Mary   Are you sure you're alright?

Anna *just nods, as* **Katherine** *begins to cry.*

Edward   What is that mewling?

He turns around and sees **Katherine.**

Edward   Are you *crying?*

Katherine   But . . .

Can you not . . .

Can you not see who I am?

Edward   Who you are?

Who you are?

What is this?

Agnes   Leave her my love –

Katherine *now loses it, fully sobbing.*

Edward   Stop it!

But she can't stop.

	I said stop it!
Joan	Agnes.
	Behave.
Edward	Right!
Elizabeth	Brother.
Edward	Out!
	Out of here!
	And Joan?
	Give her none of the meat –
	No scraps –
	No dinner at all.

Joan *pushes* **Katherine** *out of the hall, and comes back.*

Elizabeth	Where did you get this?
Agnes	I hunted it –
Edward	Oh my love –
	We don't hunt cows!
Agnes	Silly me.
Elizabeth	But all the cows are dead.
Agnes	One clearly wasn't.
Elizabeth	Tell me what this is.
Edward	It's *beef.*
Elizabeth	It can't be.
Edward	Oh Lizzie,
	No need to be jealous.

I love all my ladies equally –

Now eat up, it's getting cold.

But behind them, **Anna** *falters –*

Mary   Really Annie –

Are you OK?

Elizabeth   I won't eat this.

Edward   You won't what?

Elizabeth *stands up.*

Edward   Sit back down.

And eat your food.

Elizabeth   This is witchcraft.

Clear as day.

And **Anna** *collapses.*

Elizabeth   See?

See?

Clearly –

She snuck some of this before we did!

Joan *and* **Mary** *pull* **Anna** *up and she comes to –*

Edward   Have I wandered into the madhouse?

He turns to **Mary** *and* **Joan**.

Edward   Get her out of here!

Joan   Sorry sir –

It'll just be the –

Edward   The what?

Joan   Nothing.

Joan *and* **Mary** *help* **Anna** *out of the hall.* **Elizabeth** *grabs* **Edward**'s *plate from him.*

Elizabeth	Clearly –
	This is the work of the devil, brother.
	I cannot let you eat it.
Edward	If you don't put that down I will be very angry, Elizabeth.
	Very angry.
Elizabeth	And what will you do?
Edward	You think I don't have options.
	I have options.
Elizabeth	Really? Like what?
Edward	I'll send you to cousin Henry.
Elizabeth	You wouldn't.
Edward	Oh yes I would.
	Little Margaret needs someone to help her –
	With her needlework –
	Would you like that, sister?
Elizabeth	Maybe.
Edward	But what about little George.
	He needs a nursemaid.
	A good one.
	He's teething.
Elizabeth	You'd really send me away?
Edward	I am a man, Elizabeth.
	I need meat.

Elizabeth *throws the plate on the floor, then leaves.*

Edward   Madness.

                   Madness!

Agnes *pushes her own plate over to him, he shakes his head, and eats once again.*

Scene Five

Agnes *is now in* **Katherine**'s *room – brushing her own hair.*

Agnes   No one has been in to light my fire.

                   Are you going to let the lady of the house go
                   cold?

Elizabeth   Where did you find the cow?

Agnes   A cow, a horse.

                   Really – what's the difference?

Elizabeth   Out!

                   Get out!

Agnes   But isn't it my right –

                   As the lady of the house –

                   To make that command?

Elizabeth   No, no, no, no, no

Agnes   Aren't you tired, Elizabeth?

                   Of holding all this up by yourself –

Elizabeth *launches at her, and tries to rip the dress off her, but* **Agnes** *defends herself well.*

Agnes   I worked in the fields, sister,

                   Remember?

So now it is time for me to ask you –

What do you want?

Maybe I'll be able to grant it for you.

Elizabeth   There is nothing you could give me.

Agnes   Really?

Nothing?

What about a baby?

You brother's baby to be exact –

I think you would call it –

An heir?

Agnes *takes* **Elizabeth**'s *hand, and places it on her stomach.*

Downstairs, **Katherine**, **Joan** *and* **Mary** *now sit in the hall, with* **Edward**.

Edward   Maybe I should visit him.

The King.

Offer my services –

I could help raise an army –

He'll need one –

And I know which families to avoid.

Katherine *once again starts to cry.*

Edward   Oh Lord!

Must I always be surrounded by women!

The endless indignities!

The fits, the tears!

What must it be like in your heads?

Mary   That's not women, Sir –

That's witches.

Edward   Still with this witch?

Joan   Sir.

                I don't mean to overstep –

                But she did confess –

                In this very room –

                We all saw it –

Mary   She did, Sir.

Edward   But you trusted in a witchfinder –

                Didn't you?

                An enemy!

Joan   I know, Sir.

                We never should have trusted him.

                We should have asked you.

Edward   Yes.

                Well.

Joan   You should have examined us.

Edward   Examined you?

Joan   Yes.

                He stripped us, sir.

                To look for marks.

Edward   Well.

                Maybe I should.

                It is my role.

                Isn't it?

He walks over to **Katherine**.

Edward   You heard.

Lift your skirts.

Katherine *hesitates, and then lifts her skirt.* **Edward** *looks.*

Edward   Properly. I can't see.

She lifts more. He grabs at her.

Come on.

Further.

I bet you like this.

Devil girl.

She lifts more.

Edward   Is this a *mark*?

Katherine   No!

Edward   Agnes.

Katherine   Yes.

Edward   Is this where he suckles you?

He pinches. **Katherine** *cries out.*

Katherine   Yes.

Edward   A confession!

Mary   Shall we go?

Joan   Just a moment –

Edward   And you like it?

Katherine   Feels like kisses.

Edward   Another mark –

Even higher.

Katherine   Well he goes all the way up doesn't he . . .

Edward   Oh I bet he does –

               Here?

Katherine Higher.

Edward   Devil child.

Katherine I was.

               But he's made me a woman.

               He's made me his.

Edward   I must claim you back then.

Katherine No.

               I'm his.

His head disappears under her skirts. **Katherine** *is shocked at first, but then, delighted.*

   Mary   Joan.

               Come on.

   Joan   Alright.

They leave.

Upstairs, **Elizabeth** *and* **Agnes** *continue their discussion –*

Elizabeth It can't be.

               I don't believe it.

Agnes   But this is what you've always wanted, isn't it?

               An heir.

               Someone in the house who can carry on your name.

               Your legacy.

Elizabeth But what do you want?

Agnes   Why worry about that –

               When you can have all your dreams?

Agnes   Why worry about that –

             When you can have all your dreams?

Elizabeth   Because every day I worry –

             Every dream I have ever had –

             Has gone into these walls –

             So any disturbance –

             Any at all –

             I worry –

             And today –

             That is you.

Agnes   But Elizabeth –

             What more can I do –

             To prove to you that this is who I am –

             Where I belong?

Elizabeth   You'll never!

Agnes   I am not here to steal it from you!

             What I want is to help you build it –

             What we both want –

             Raise the heir we both need –

             I can do it without you –

             But I would prefer to do it with you.

A scream! Downstairs, **Joan** *runs into the hall, covered in blood,*
disturbing **Edward** *and* **Katherine**, **Mary** *behind her.*

Elizabeth   What's happened?

Joan   She's dead!

             She'd dead!

Edward   Who?

Agnes *and* **Elizabeth** *run into the room.*

Joan   Anna –

                She had pains at dinner –

                And I sent her down and and –

                She was

                She was –

                She –

                She's dead.

Edward   Anna, *dead*?

Mary *hugs* **Joan**.

Elizabeth   Alright.

                It's alright –

Joan *breaks away from* **Mary** *and points at* **Katherine**.

Joan   She killed her!

                She killed her she killed her she killed her –

                I've told you and told you –

                And you didn't listen!

                And now she killed her –

                You killed her!

She launches at **Katherine** –

Katherine   I didn't!

                It's not me!

                I'm not her!

Katherine *looks over at* **Elizabeth**.

Edward   What?

But then **Joan** *sees . . .*

Joan   No –

It's not –

No –

But it was you . . .

Joan *turns to* **Agnes**.

Joan   You gave her that drink.

Agnes *tuns to* **Elizabeth**.

Agnes   Sister, what do you think?

Mary *looks at* **Agnes**.

Mary   That bottle.

That's what killed here.

Agnes   Agnes gave it to me –

Didn't you?

Katherine   No!

Mary   Did she?

Katherine   Sister –

Sister – help me –

Please?

Joan   Why are you calling her that . . .

Agnes   *What do you think, sister?*

Elizabeth *looks at* **Agnes**. *She thinks. Then she looks at* **Katherine** . . .

Elizabeth   Yes, this is her – this is the witch!

Joan   I knew it!

Katherine	No!
	I'm not!
	I'm not!
	It's her!
Edward	She just confessed!
	Right here!
Joan	She's evil –
	Hang her!
	Cut her!
	Don't spare a single nail!
Katherine	No – please –
	My love –
	Don't you see?
	Don't you see who I am?
	We've just started our life together!
	You finally want me!
	As your wife –
Edward	My wife?

He slaps her, and **Katherine** *turns on* **Agnes** *– hitting her.*

Katherine	You devil!
	You monster!
	This is the witch –
	This is her!

Edward *pulls her off* **Agnes** –

Edward	Are you alright, my love?

Agnes   Yes.

But I hope . . .

Well, I hope the baby is . . .

Edward   The what?

Agnes   My love, I'm pregnant.

Edward *looks confused for a second, but* **Agnes** *places his hand on her stomach.*

Agnes   See?

Edward   A miracle!

It's a miracle!

Katherine   NO!

Edward *picks* **Agnes** *up and kisses her.*

Edward   Oh my love!

My love!

Agnes   It's a boy!

Edward   A boy!

God works in mysterious ways –

But he has saved us all!

Katherine   No! Please –

No!

Edward *grabs her – but* **Agnes** *pulls him back.*

Agnes   A moment my love –

I wish to say goodbye –

She then speaks to **Katherine** *privately . . .*

Agnes   I am sorry, Katherine –

Really, I am.

But think about it –

I've worn your name for only a day –

And already –

I've done all you couldn't.

Who is more you than me?

But from one old friend to another –

I am sorry.

Agnes *kisses her on the forehead, and* **Edward** *and* **Joan** *drag* **Katherine** *away kicking and screaming . . .*

And soon, **Katherine** *is hung . . .*

Act V

Scene One

A finished feast is laid out across the table. **Edward** *is dressed in full armour, with his friend* **Francis** – *a general.* **Edward** *and* **Francis** *hold muskets and practise shooting.* **Agnes** *and* **Elizabeth** *sit at the table,* **Mary** *and* **Joan** *serve them.*

Francis *shoots.* **Edward** *cheers.* **Edward** *takes the gun and starts to load it.*

Elizabeth	Mary –
	Did the cooks confirm the stocks in the larder?
Mary	He said we have enough for three weeks.
Elizabeth	We need more.
	Francis, what did you hear of the Vernays?
	Is it true?
Francis	What did you hear?
Elizabeth	That soldiers came in –
	Ripped the garments off their priest –
	And smashed their organ –
	Is it really happening like that?
Francis	This is who we're fighting –
	You should read some of the pamphlets circulating in their camps.
	These people –
	And I do mean *people* –
	For the women preach as much as the men –

> They say a person can pray as just as well in a field as in a church –
>
> And so they wish to tear down the church –
>
> And soon they'll tear down the taverns –
>
> And the houses –
>
> And let the grass grow on the streets –
>
> Because they want it all wiped away –
>
> To start again.

Edward   But can they *fight?*

What should I expect tomorrow?

Francis   Haven't had the joy of facing them yet.

Edward *points the musket at* **Mary***, jokingly.*

Edward   Of course!

They're always run, run, running away from battle!

Elizabeth   Edward.

Please.

Edward *holds out the gun for* **Elizabeth***.*

Edward   Have a go, Lizzie!

Elizabeth   *Oh, Edward.*

Edward *holds out the musket for* **Agnes***.*

Edward   My love?

Elizabeth   No, Edward –

You need to practise!

But **Agnes** *takes the musket from him.*

Edward   Be careful now –

Because if you're too good we'll have to take you along tomorrow.

Edward *laughs,* **Agnes** *shoots. She is good.* **Francis** *cheers.*

Francis   Edward's right.

                     We will be needing you tomorrow.

Agnes   So nervous you're recruiting women now?

Francis *hands* **Edward** *a glass.*

Francis   If you can hit this –

                     I'll give you Edward's spot.

Edward   Francis!

Elizabeth   *Don't.*

Francis   The skill isn't just in shooting –

                     But getting shot.

                     Isn't that right, Eddie?

Francis *helps* **Agnes** *aim the musket.* **Edward** *holds the glass away from him. She shoots and hits the target.* **Francis** *cheers,*

Francis   I have a little spot right at the back of my
                     horse.

                     What do you think?

Agnes   I think I'd like my own horse, at least.

In the background, a baby cries.

Agnes   *Joan?*

Joan   On my way, Mistress.

Joan *leaves.*

Elizabeth   Maybe everyone should go to bed.

Edward   True warriors don't sleep before battle –

                     Isn't that right, Francis?

Elizabeth   Sister?

                     Bed.

Agnes   But what if I'm a true warrior?

Francis   Then we must make sure you choose our side.

Agnes   Alright then.

               Recruit me.

               Why should I offer my superior skills to the King?

Edward   Because he is the King.

               My love.

               Our King.

               That is all.

Agnes   I'm afraid I need more.

Francis   Fight for him, because he will win.

Agnes   But will he?

Edward   He has God on his side.

Agnes   You really believe God supports the King?

Edward   God made the King.

               God chose the King.

Agnes   If God built a man to lead over other men –

               Wouldn't he make that man better than other men –

Edward   And *he did*.

The baby cries once again.

Agnes   Mary.

               Please?

Mary   Yes, Mistress.

Mary *leaves.*

Elizabeth	Why don't you go with her, sister?
Agnes	The King is weak.
Francis	Edward –
	This is really how you talk at the table?
Agnes	You know he is!
Edward	*Kitty.*
Agnes	You see him fail at every juncture –
	And because of those failures –
	You will stand tomorrow –
	Risking your life –
	And your men's lives –
	Because the King lost control of his subjects.
Francis	The King has made mistakes –
	But a King is not really the man –
	A King is, well.
	A cursory glance might suggest –
	That a King is the top stone of the pyramid –
	But no –
	A King is really the keystone of the bridge –
	Not an ornament at the top –
	But the foundation.
	Without it –
	Chaos.

Elizabeth *takes* **Agnes** *away.*

Elizabeth	Behave.
	I know you like your jokes but –

Agnes   I wasn't joking.

Elizabeth   Then I hope there's still time to fit your
armour.

Agnes   They're going to lose.

Elizabeth   I know they seem rather flippant this evening –

But that's the only way to not fall apart.

I promise –

Underneath –

They are serious.

And they will win.

Agnes   And what then?

Elizabeth   I have to get back.

Agnes   No.

Tell me.

Imagine.

The war is won.

What's next?

Elizabeth   Let's try and win it first, shall we?

Agnes   Answer me!

Elizabeth   This!

Agnes   This house?

Elizabeth   Yes.

This house.

This house is next –

This house is forever –

Agnes   I see.

Elizabeth	And what about this surprises you?
Agnes	It is just bricks!
	Bricks that boast one skill –
	And one skill only –
	That they don't fall down!
Elizabeth	For bricks?
	I think that means a lot.
Agnes	A lot, yes.
	But not *more*.
	Because what does it do?
	What does it change?
Elizabeth	Nothing.
	It changes, does nothing.
	It exists –
	It simply is.
	That is all.
	And that is *everything!*
Agnes	*Is it?*
Elizabeth	How can you make it sound so small?
	Think about its position –
	On top of a hill.
	Visible for miles –
	A solid point on the horizon –
	Through which people know where they are –
	Farmers –

Knowing the rain is an hour away when it hits
us –

Workers –

Seeing the sun fall behind our roof and
knowing –

It is an hour till freedom –

Travellers –

Seeing us and knowing they are finally close to
home –

The light from our windows guiding them –

Back to the warmth of their own walls –

And inside it's even better –

Every person for miles can find employment
here –

Employment that their parents held –

And their parents before them –

And so on and so on and so on –

Stretching back hundreds of years –

Safety.

Not just in wages –

But the deep belief in their bones –

That because it has stretched so far back –

It must stretch so far forward also –

Today –

And forever –

For their children –

And their children's children –

Agnes   Oh Elizabeth –

All this duty!

It's holding you down.

Elizabeth   I like duty.

Agnes   But look at yourself!

You are the woman who turned to blood and poison –

Who bared her own wrist for the knife –

Think of what you could be if you just let it all go?

Think about it –

What do you want?

You –

Elizabeth –

Elizabeth   Years ago I put away all those wants –

Agnes   Then pull them out again!

Think about it –

We could leave here –

Elizabeth   Leave?

And go where?

Agnes   Anywhere!

And we could do anything!

Elizabeth   When I was your age I thought the same.

I schemed and flirted my way through London –

Nothing, no one ever enough –

Needing more, more and more –

But then I came home.

And after years away the house was completely unchanged –

From the day I left it.

And in that I finally found contentment –

And that's what you need now.

Agnes   You who taught me desire –

Now preach restraint?

Elizabeth   You say this house changes nothing –

What is it you want to change?

You say we should leave here –

Leave here to do what?

Agnes   I don't know!

I don't know –

But I will know when I see it –

I have to.

For everything I did to get here –

There has to be more.

Elizabeth   Remember when we first met?

You were so dedicated –

So proud –

You had moulded yourself under God –

And that made you strong, yes –

But all that focus and discipline –

It also made you content –

Didn't it?

Find that again.

Agnes   But how?

I was good.

I was good!

Elizabeth You should get into bed –

And cry into your pillow –

Get it all out –

Scream if you need to.

Then sleep.

And tomorrow when you watch two men ride out to war –

It will put everything in its place –

I promise.

The baby cries once again.

Agnes   Joan?

Mary?

JOAN.

Scene Two

Edward *visits* **Agnes** *before battle, she is in bed. He is half dressed in his armour.*

Edward   My love?

Are you awake?

Agnes *sits up.*

Edward   I wanted to reassure you.

Today.

It will all be fine.

Francis is a great general –

And we will come out victorious.

Agnes   I am sure, my love.

Edward   Francis seemed confident –

Didn't he?

Agnes   Very.

Edward   Not scared?

Agnes   I don't think so.

Edward   Isn't it mad that in a few hours I will ride into battle!

–

Is it –

Mad –

Though?

It's the King.

Our King!

I would –

Have always done everything I can to defend the King.

But.

But.

He could lose.

And if he does lose –

Then.

Then.

Tell me to be brave.

Agnes   As you say –

             You have always done everything –

             Everything to protect the King.

Edward   It's been years.

             Years since Francis has been here –

             And one visit –

             One visit and here I am.

             Fitting my armour.

Agnes   You're loyal.

Edward   Oh so loyal.

             Passed over –

             Seen through –

             You know I see it now –

             Since school –

             I've just been tagging along behind that man –

             And the rest of them –

             I didn't carry his books for him –

             But I may as well have done.

             And then he comes here –

             One rainy day.

             He'd fallen out of favour –

             And he needed men to win it back –

             And who has men?

             I have men!

             I could have demanded things.

Why didn't I?

I just said yes.

Yes, Francis –

Whatever you need!

I should have made a list.

I should have said no.

Maybe I still could.

Do you think I could?

We could simply –

Not go tomorrow.

Happens all the time –

Men change their minds!

Don't they?

We could do that –

Couldn't we?

Agnes   And then what would we do?

Edward   Let the war end and see what's left.

Agnes   It will be a new world –

Edward   I'm scared.

That's what's happening –

Nothing more –

Don't worry my love –

I'll fight for you today –

I'll be brave –

We'll win –

And then I swear it –

This house and our family –

It'll stand for a thousand years.

Everything as it should be.

Edward *stands up and starts to finish dressing himself.*

Agnes *reluctantly helps him. Then she has an idea, and gets a necklace. She kisses it, and puts it around his neck.*

Agnes   Good luck –

From me.

Edward *kisses it.*

Edward   I will wear it with pride.

Elizabeth *comes in.*

Elizabeth   Brother?

Are you ready?

He nods. They hug. He leaves. **Elizabeth** *stands with* **Agnes**.

Elizabeth   You see.

You feel better, don't you?

Agnes   Yes.

Much better.

Scene Three

Edward *returns from battle. He is seriously wounded, and bleeding heavily. He is held up by* **Mary** *and* **Joan**.

Edward   Katherine –

KATHERINE!

Elizabeth *meets him.* **Joan** *and* **Mary** *lay him down and try to dress his wounds.*

Elizabeth   Brother –

Brother!

Elizabeth *takes over from* **Joan** *and* **Mary**.

Elizabeth   Where is Francis?

Edward *shakes his head*.

Edward   They are coming.

I've drawn up the bridge –

They'll surround us.

You have to.

Elizabeth   I know, I know.

I can do it.

I'll keep them out.

Oh Edward –

Edward   Where is she?

Where's Kitty?

Where's my son?

Elizabeth   Mary –

Fetch little Edward –

Edward   And Katherine?

Elizabeth   And Katherine.

Edward   You'll keep them out?

Elizabeth   I'll keep them out.

Edward   Think on it –

My son growing up in a siege!

He'll be so strong.

Elizabeth   There's never been stronger.

Agnes *comes in.*

Edward   My love!

My love.

You'll tell him about this?

Little Edward.

You'll tell him?

Agnes   Tell him what?

Edward   This!

The battle –

Me –

Leading.

Elizabeth   We'll tell him.

Edward   He'll know.

He'll always know.

Edward *dies.* **Elizabeth** *takes a moment, and then stands up. She starts to hand muskets out to* **Mary**, **Joan** *and* **Agnes**.

Elizabeth   Joan –

The bridge is up but it must be secured –

Any men who've come back –

That's their duty.

And Mary –

Head to the larder, count everything –

Then lock it.

No.

Lock it first.

Both of you –

Anyone coming back from battle –

They must be assessed –

Sister –

You will gather anything that can be used to treat them –

We need them ready to fight –

Well?

Everyone clear?

Joan *and* **Mary** *nod.* **Elizabeth** *waits on* **Agnes**.

Elizabeth	Sister?
	Do you hear me?
Agnes	You didn't give me a reason.
	I asked.
	And there was nothing.
Elizabeth	Stop this.
	Stop it!
	You've had your tantrums –
	But this is not the time.
	There are men outside who wish to pull this house down –
	And kill us all.
Agnes	But it is time –
	Isn't it –
	Don't you think?
Elizabeth	Joan.
	Mary.

	Go.
Agnes	No.
	Both of you.
	What do you think –
	Is it time this house was torn down?
Joan	My Lady –
	No!
Agnes	Forget duty, Joan –
	I release you –
	Both of you.
	Surrender –
	Save yourselves.
Elizabeth	Don't listen to her.
Joan	Mistress, I would never.
Agnes	And why not?
Joan	My Lady –
	I'm loyal!
	Don't you know that?

Agnes *looks at* **Mary**.

Agnes	And you?
Mary	My Lady.
	I'd rather stay here.
	It's safer, here.
	Isn't it?
Agnes	I am Agnes!

Mary   Mistress?

Agnes   I am the witch!

                I killed Anna!

                I stole Katherine's life!

Joan   But –

Agnes   And I –

                The witch Agnes –

                I have been your mistress –

Elizabeth   We don't have time –

Agnes   And the Lady Elizabeth has known this –

                She wanted it!

                These are the women you serve –

                Murderers and witches!

Elizabeth   Lies.

Joan   My Lady –

                You're scared.

                That's fine.

                We're all scared –

Agnes *points the musket at both* **Joan** *and* **Mary**.

Agnes   Run.

Joan *and* **Mary** *run away.*

Elizabeth   You know if we were to open those gates –

                We would be flooded with men like that Witchfinder –

                Is that who you fight for?

Agnes   I don't care, Elizabeth!

                I don't care –

I only know that those men will tear this house down –

And I'll help them.

Elizabeth   And what will happen without this house?

People won't be able to find their way home in the dark.

Agnes   Then –

Then let them stumble in the dark –

As I did –

Yes –

I spent a lifetime in the dark –

So let them stumble around –

And see if they make it into the light –

Elizabeth   And if they don't?

Agnes   If they don't,

Well –

They don't!

And if they do –

Then –

Then they'll have earned everything they can get their hands on –

Elizabeth   That is chaos!

Agnes   Isn't that what we need?

Elizabeth   Because they aren't just coming for the King –

They are coming for all of us –

Our hearts and our minds –

They'll call you evil, Agnes –

They will –

Because they're coming for everything –

For every word out of our mouths –

And every one that goes through our heads –

They want it all!

Agnes   As do you.

Elizabeth   I let people be as they are.

Agnes   As long as they're serving you.

They might want our minds –

But you want our bodies.

But no more –

It's over, Elizabeth.

Elizabeth   You won't do this.

Agnes   It is done.

Elizabeth   This is a tantrum.

You love this house.

I saw your eyes the first moment you stepped through that door –

And every morning since.

You'd never hurt it.

Agnes   Let's see –

How would it go?

It would start with the ropes, wouldn't it?

The ones holding up the bridge.

Snap!

Elizabeth   They wouldn't.

Agnes   The men hold on –

But the bridge is too heavy.

The ropes slip through their fingers.

And crash!

The bridge comes down.

A crash.

Elizabeth   I don't believe it.

Agnes   And over they run.

Elizabeth   You can't.

Agnes   Listen.

Pounding footsteps . . .

Elizabeth   No.

Agnes   It is time, sister.

Elizabeth *attacks* **Agnes**. **Agnes** *fights back, and wins. Stabbing* **Elizabeth**. **Elizabeth** *holds onto her.*

Elizabeth   Look around you!

Go on.

Look.

Agnes *looks around at the wall.*

Elizabeth   Heaven –

Isn't it?

Elizabeth *dies.* **Agnes** *lowers her to the floor. Then she stands up, and looks around the room. She hears footsteps. She picks up a musket.*

A **Parliamentarian** *enters to room (played by the* **Devil***). He sees her, she sees him . . . They stare at each other . . .*

Printed in the USA
CPSIA information can be obtained
at www.ICGtesting.com
LVHW022008260424
778553LV00001B/180